Whatcom County with Kids

Places to Go
and
Things to Do

Dana Rozier

Whatcom County with Kids:
Places to Go and Things to Do

© Copyright 1999 by Dana Rozier
All rights reserved.

ISBN # 0-9670750-0-9

Photograph on front cover by Mary Hogan Camp.
All others by author except where noted.

Cover design by Rod Burton at Pyramid Productions.

Maps drawn by Bob Lindquist.

Designed and published by Coho Press,
Bellingham, Washington.
Manufactured in the United States.

Front Cover: Beach on west side of Lummi Island

Contents

Notes About This Book

Area Code
The area code for Whatcom County is 360.

Everything changes!
The information in this book was accurate when it went to press. However, businesses close, prices go up, hours fluctuate. To ensure a smooth outing, please call ahead to confirm details.

Comments/Opinions
If you'd like to comment on any of the places listed in this book or let me know about a place or activity that should be included in the next edition, please write to me. I'd love to hear from you.

—Dana Rozier

Coho Press
PO Box 4428
Bellingham, WA 98227

Introduction

A few years ago when my daughter was a toddler, I went to Bellingham's Village Books to buy a parent guide for Whatcom County. I wanted a book that described interesting places and activities for families with kids in our area. Where could we go today? What could we do? When I discovered such a book didn't exist, I decided to write *Whatcom County with Kids*.

I've had a lot of fun working on this book. It's given me the opportunity to explore places and pursue activities I might otherwise not have. I've been to every park in Whatcom County, went on my first whale watch, and donned ice skates for the first time in twenty years. Most of the places I researched were worthwhile, but some were not. In this book I only included places that I thought were interesting, educational, or just plain fun. Many of the activities listed are free or cost little money. Maps, driving directions, addresses, and phone numbers are also included. I wrote the kind of book that would be useful to me as a parent. I hope it's useful to you and that you use this book as a guide to get out and explore Whatcom County with kids.

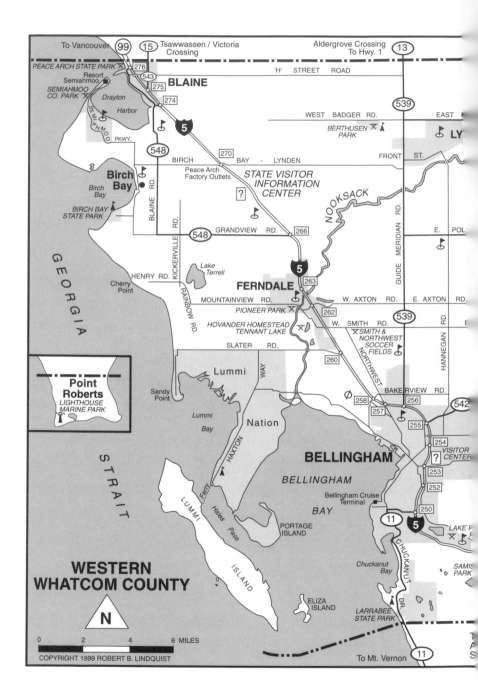

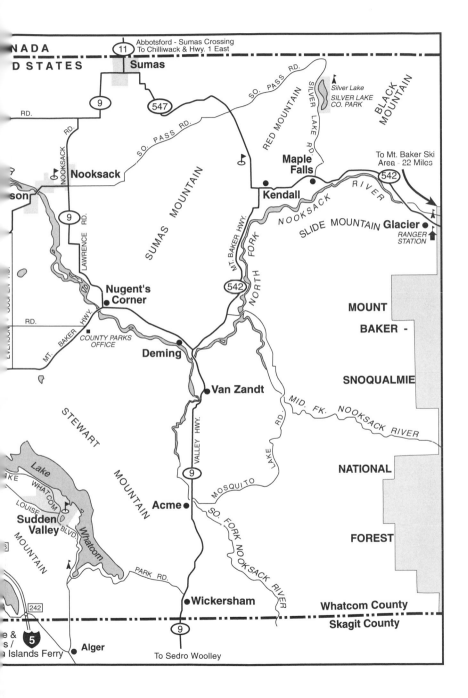

NADA

D STATES

Sumas

Abbotsford - Sumas Crossing
11 To Chilliwack & Hwy. 1 East

9
547
RD.

SO. PASS RD.

SO. PASS RD.

NOOKSACK RD.

SO. PASS RD.

RED MOUNTAIN

SILVER LAKE

SILVER LAKE RD.

Silver Lake

SILVER LAKE
CO. PARK

BLACK MOUNTAIN

Nooksack

SUMAS MOUNTAIN

Maple Falls

Kendall

To Mt. Baker Ski
Area - 22 Miles

542

RIVER

NOOKSACK

son

9

LAWRENCE RD.

MT. BAKER HWY.

NORTH FORK

SLIDE MOUNTAIN **Glacier**

RANGER
STATION

Nugent's Corner

RD.

MT. BAKER HWY.

COUNTY PARKS
OFFICE

Deming

542

NORTH

MOUNT

BAKER -

Van Zandt

VALLEY HWY.

MID. FK. NOOKSACK RIVER

LAKE RD.

SNOQUALMIE

STEWART

MOUNTAIN

Lake

WHATCOM

LOUISE

Sudden Valley

BLVD.

Whatcom

9

MOSQUITO

Acme

SO. FORK

NOOKSACK RIVER

NATIONAL

MOUNTAIN

242

PARK RD.

Wickersham

Whatcom County

Skagit County

FOREST

e &
s /
Islands Ferry

5

Alger

9

To Sedro Woolley

7

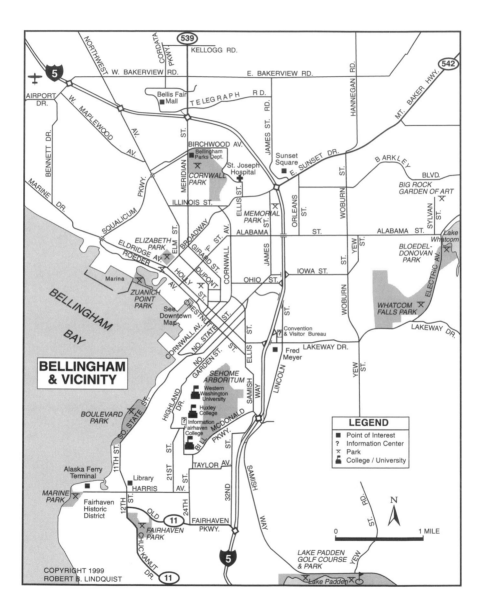

BELLINGHAM
& VICINITY

LEGEND

■ Point of Interest
? Information Center
✕ Park
♦ College / University

N

0   1 MILE

COPYRIGHT 1999
ROBERT B. LINDQUIST

8

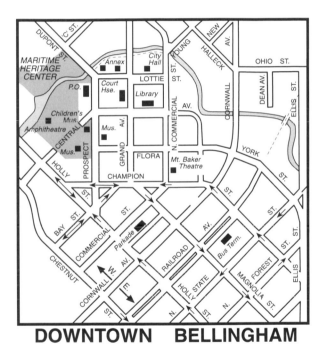

DOWNTOWN BELLINGHAM

Bellingham Parks

Within the city of Bellingham there are over twenty-five parks, and each one offers families something unique. Head to Boulevard Park to watch sunsets and to stroll along the water. If you're in the mood for some exercise, go to Lake Padden and walk the 2.8 mile loop around the lake. On Thursday evenings in the summer, pack a picnic dinner and travel to Elizabeth Park to enjoy an outdoor concert.

The maps on pages 8 and 9 show the location of the major parks in Bellingham.

COMMUNITY PARKS

These large parks managed by the Bellingham Parks and Recreation Department offer a variety of activities.

Bloedel Donovan Park

2214 Electric Ave., Bellingham; 676-6985

Feature Highlights: boat launch, multipurpose building, playground, restrooms, sandy swimming beach. **Seasonal:** boat rental, concession stand, putt-putt golf course, sandy volleyball court

This park, once a lumberyard for the Bloedel Mill, is located right on Lake Whatcom, and many activities center around the lake. The large swimming area has a sandy beach and is staffed by lifeguards in the summer. Fishing and boating are popular and a boat launch is available at the north end of the park. During the summer, non-motorized boats such as canoes, kayaks, or paddleboats are available to rent. A concession stand, eighteen hole putt-putt golf course, and volleyball court are also open in the summer.

The playground at Bloedel Donovan is scheduled for new play equipment which should be installed by the time you read this book. The multipurpose building at Bloedel Donovan hosts many community events. Parents of preschoolers might be interested in two programs that are held in this building. Kindergym and Toddler Time, run by the Bellingham Parks and Recreation Office, provide parents with the opportunity to chat while their children play. To read more about these programs look in Chapter 5, Indoor Activities.

Boulevard Park

S. State St. and Bayview Dr., Bellingham; 676-6985

Feature Highlights: beaches, boardwalk, family concerts in the summer, kite flying, paved trail along Bellingham Bay, play structure, restrooms, sculptures, sunsets, water views

The charm of Boulevard Park is in its location right on Bellingham Bay. Across the water you can see Lummi Island to the west, the port of Bellingham and Squalicum Harbor to the north, and the ferry terminal in Fairhaven to the south. People like to walk, jog, or rollerblade on the paved trail along the water's edge and along the boardwalk at the south end of the park. The frequent breezes off the bay also make the park a popular place to fly kites. A big piece of play equipment in the shape of a boat is a wonderful place for young children to climb, slide, or pretend to be captain of the ship. There are a couple of small beaches on the north and south ends of the park that are good places to dig in the sand or look for interesting shells and rocks. In the summer, Boulevard Park hosts outdoor family music concerts on Saturday evenings. Call the Bellingham Parks and Recreation Office, 676-6985, for a list of programs and starting times.

Boardwalk at Boulevard Park

13

Cornwall Park

2800 Cornwall Ave., Bellingham; 676-6985

Feature Highlights: basketball court, picnic shelters, playgrounds, restrooms, rose garden, Squalicum Creek, tennis courts, trails, wading pool (summer only)

On sunny summer afternoons the wading pool at Cornwall Park is a popular place for young children and their families. The pool has a gated fence around it so you don't have to worry about your toddler scampering off. Inside the gated area are benches and enough concrete area to accommodate many families with strollers, towels, water toys, and backpacks. The pool is designed for children six years old and younger. It is open every day in the summer from 11am to 6pm and a lifeguard is on duty.

Picnic shelters, restrooms, and a playground are located near the wading pool. The playground features climbing equipment, slides, and both baby swings and regular swings. New equipment is scheduled to be installed by the summer of 1999. Squalicum Creek runs behind the playground and is a favorite place for older kids to explore. Returning salmon are sometimes seen in the creek during the fall.

This sixty-five acre park also features large grassy areas, shaded hiking trails, a 1.8 mile fitness trail, tennis and basketball courts, another smaller playground, and a rose garden.

Since this park is so large it has three entrances: two are off Meridian Street, and one is off Cornwall Avenue. To reach the wading pool and nearby playground, use the northern Meridian Street entrance. Here you'll also find the office to the Bellingham Parks and Recreation Department, an excellent resource to learn more about our area's parks, trails, and seasonal activities for kids. To reach the beginning of the 1.8 mile fitness trail or the basketball and tennis courts, use the southern Meridian Street entrance. If you enter the park from the Cornwall Avenue entrance, you can reach another playground and some horseshoe pits. Trails connect all areas of the park. The rose garden is planted near the entrance off Cornwall Avenue and features over one hundred varieties of roses.

Fairhaven Park
107 Chuckanut Dr., Bellingham; 676-6985

Feature Highlights: basketball court, Padden Creek, picnic shelters, playground, restrooms, tennis courts, trails, wading pool (summers only)

Fairhaven Park offers a range of activities for the whole family. Every day during the summer, from 11am to 6pm, its popular wading pool is open to children six years old and younger. A lifeguard is on duty. Near the wading pool are two different playgrounds. One is designed for preschoolers; it has baby swings and regular swings, and metal animals on which to ride. The other playground has plenty of regular swings and a wooden climbing structure with slides. Fairhaven Park also has tennis and basketball courts, and big, grassy fields. Behind the tennis courts and down the stairs is Padden Creek. This shallow creek is a shady place to explore in the summer and an excellent place to watch salmon in the fall. Fairhaven Park's lovely rose garden was devastated by hungry deer in 1998. Plans are in the works to replace the roses and to build new fences that will, everyone hopes, keep the deer out.

Lake Padden Park
4882 Samish Way, Bellingham; 676-6985

Feature Highlights: boat launch, boat rentals (summer only), fishing piers, picnic shelters, playground, restrooms, swimming area, tennis courts, trail around lake

At 1008 acres, Lake Padden Park is by far Bellingham's largest park. One of the most popular activities is to jog or walk the 2.8 mile loop around the lake. The mostly flat, well maintained trail meanders through grassy areas and forest. Since this trail isn't paved the whole way, jogging strollers work best on its surface. Visitors can access the trail from any of Lake Padden's parking lots.

A terrific playground for toddlers is located on the south end of the lake. The climbing toy is scaled to their size and a shallow ramp leads up to the slide. Next to this playground is an area designed for older kids. It has a tire swing and a tall, twisty slide. Both baby swings and regular swings are available. This sunny playground by the lake is a favorite place for toddler play groups to meet. Use the East Entrance off Samish Way to reach the playground.

When the weather warms up, Lake Padden is a popular swimming and sunbathing spot. Lifeguards are on duty from mid-June through Labor Day. Non-motorized boats, such as lake kayaks and canoes, are for rent during the summer. Use the West Entrance off Samish Way to reach the swimming area and boat rentals.

Lake Padden is always a busy place on the opening day of fishing. People stand on the shore or row out on the water hoping to catch one of the many trout that have been released into the lake. Fishing licenses aren't required for children fourteen years old and under. Use the East Entrance to reach the boat launch.

Falls along Whatcom Creek at Maritime Heritage Center

Maritime Heritage Center
1600 C St., Bellingham; 676-6806

Feature Highlights: hillclimb, salmon life cycle facility, stream restoration site, trails

This usually quiet park fills with activity in the fall when returning Chinook, Coho, and Chum salmon arrive to spawn. Area residents line up along Whatcom Creek to watch these magnificent fish or to try their luck at catching one. Fishing is allowed along the creek.

A good place to see the fish up close is in the Adult Holding Pond which is a part of the hatchery facility. This cement pond is located near the parking lot on C Street. A word of caution for parents: Since this is a working hatchery that needs eggs and milt to hatch new salmon, the fish do get killed here. They are bonked on the head. My oldest child would be horrified to see this event even if I explained to her that the salmon are at the end of their life

17

cycle and would die anyway after spawning. Luckily, on the days we were there, the hatchery was pretty quiet and we just got to marvel at those fish. You can call the Center to see on which days the fish will be bonked. Usually, it's only a couple of days a week.

When the park is quiet again, Maritime Heritage is a lovely place to walk along the trails through the stream restoration site. This area used to be a city dump and blackberry patch. Volunteers have spent countless hours clearing debris and planting native plants along the creek to create diverse habitats. Before you leave the park, be sure to visit the beautiful thirty foot totem pole recounting the legend of Salmon Woman.

As this book is being completed, workers are finishing the hillclimb, a wide set of stairs that will take visitors from the park to the area behind Whatcom Museum. The locally renowned Shrimp Shack restaurant has been purchased and will be demolished to expand the park.

Whatcom Falls Park
1401 Electric Ave., Bellingham; 676-6985

Feature Highlights: basketball court, fish hatchery, fishing, picnic shelters, playgrounds, restrooms, tennis courts, trails

At 241 acres, Whatcom Falls Park is the second largest park in Bellingham. Within the park, families can walk the shady trails along Whatcom Creek, fish from its banks, or view the many waterfalls along the creek. Take in the sound and spray from a large waterfall from the handsome stone bridge that was constructed in 1939 by the Works Progress Administration. To reach the bridge, park in the lower lot (use the entrance off Lakeway Drive) and follow the asphalt path to the creek. From this lower parking lot, families are also closer to the preschool playground and to the fish hatchery. The preschool playground has baby swings, a twisty slide, a metal climbing dome, and metal animals on which to ride. The Bellingham Trout Hatchery, located nearby, raises trout to stock area lakes and streams. It is open to the public every day from 8am to 5pm. Visitors can watch the small trout swimming in their rearing pens and learn more about the fish hatchery by reading the informational displays.

From the park's upper parking lot (use the entrance off Electric Avenue) families are closer to the tennis and basketball courts and the big kid playground. This playground has a wooden climbing structure and swings. If you walk down the paved road behind the swings, you will come to the children's fishing pond which is stocked with trout raised from the nearby hatchery. Kids fourteen and under can fish there for free and without a license.

WPA Bridge at Whatcom Falls Park

19

NEIGHBORHOOD PARKS

No matter where you live in Bellingham, there's sure to be a neighborhood park nearby. If you'd like a change of scenery from your local park, try one of the sixteen listed below. For more information about any of these parks, contact the Bellingham Parks and Recreation Department at 676-6985.

Big Rock Park
Sylvan St. & Illinois Ln.

This nine acre park was once a nursery and is now a shady retreat with rhododendrons, Japanese maples, sculptures, and picnic areas that overlook Lake Whatcom.

Birchwood Park
2709 Cedarwood Ave.

This brand new neighborhood park, scheduled to open by the summer of 1999, will have a playground, basketball court, and a play field.

Broadway Park
Cornwall Ave. & N. Park Dr.

Broadway is a sunny park with fields, restrooms, basketball courts, a climbing structure with a slide, a tire swing, and both baby swings and regular swings.

Carl Lobe Park
Eldridge Ave. & Victor St.

This triangular park has one baby and one regular swing, metal animals on which to ride, a metal engine and caboose to climb or sit on, and a small field with a backstop.

Cornwall Tot Lot
Cornwall St. & D St.

This small park is located on a busy street, but is designed especially for toddlers. A cyclone fence surrounds the park. Inside families will find a climbing structure, a couple of metal animals on which to ride, and two baby swings.

Elizabeth Park
Elizabeth St. & Madison St.

Elizabeth Park, located in the historic Eldridge neighborhood, is one of Bellingham's biggest and most beautiful neighborhood parks. Captain Henry Roeder,

Gazebo at Elizabeth Park

21

an early pioneer, donated this land in the late 1800s in honor of his wife, Elizabeth. Its 4.5 acres are dotted with mature trees that provide wonderful shade during hot weather. This park features a basketball court, a fountain, a gazebo, tennis courts, and a playground with lots of swings. The playground is scheduled to be upgraded in 1999.

During the summer, Elizabeth Park hosts a Music in the Park series on Thursday evenings from 6-8pm. The music is performed in the gazebo and is paid for by funds from the Eldridge Historical Society. Call 676-6985 for more information about this summer's series.

Fouts Park
G St. & Ellsworth St.

This small park has brand new play equipment which includes a climbing structure and three different kinds of slides.

Forest and Cedar Park
Forest St. & Cedar St.

Located near the University this park features baby swings and regular swings, a basketball court, a climbing structure with slides, a large field, and restrooms.

Franklin Park
1201 Franklin St.

Franklin Park has a basketball court, a large field, and a playground with baby swings, regular swings, and a climbing structure with slides.

Highland Park
2800 Vining St.

This park on Alabama Hill has a basketball court and a small playground for preschoolers which features baby and big kid swings, a metal climbing dome, metal animals on which to ride, and a slide. Visitors have a view of Bellingham Bay over the neighborhood roofs.

Laurel Park
Indian St. & Laurel St.

My husband and I lived near this park when we were going to college. It used to be one, big grassy field. As I write this book, Laurel Park is being upgraded and now has a brand new basketball court and play equipment. The equipment includes a climbing structure, monkey bars, and three different slides. Between the nearby houses, visitors have views of Bellingham Bay to the west, and on clear days, the tip of Mt. Baker to the east.

Playground at Laurel Park

23

Lorraine Ellis Park

Ellis/Lorraine Ct. & Illinois St.

This small park in a shady cul-de-sac has a climbing structure with slides, one of which is quite tall.

Ridgemont Park

800 38th St.

This quiet park in the Ridgemont neighborhood has newer play equipment which features a large climbing structure with three slides and a set of monkey bars. It also has a basketball court, grassy areas, and one baby and one regular swing.

Roosevelt Park

2200 Verona St.

At nine acres, Roosevelt is one of the largest neighborhood parks in Bellingham. It has basketball courts, large fields, and restrooms. The playground has baby swings, regular swings, climbing equipment, slides, and a purple metal dinosaur on which to ride.

St. Clair Park

2000 St. Clair St.

From the parking lot at St. Clair Park, you can see the large fields and the building which houses the restrooms. You can also see the preschool playground with its baby swings, regular swings, metal climbing dome, metal animals on which to ride, and its slide. But there's more to the park than meets the eye. From the parking lot, you *can't* see the really cool metal slide that takes you through a short concrete culvert and pops you out at another playground below. This lower playground can also be reached by going down a set of stairs. It has a wooden climbing structure with a slide and tire swings.

Sunnyland Memorial Park
Illinois St. & King St.

Part of this five acre park lies behind Sunnyland Elementary. When school is in session, visitors may use the large, grassy areas within the park, but should stay off the play equipment. Students at Sunnyland have the use of it during school hours, 8am-4pm. The equipment includes a climbing structure, a very tall twisty slide, and a tire swing. Our family likes to come here to play and then walk the Railroad Trail to Barkley Village for a snack. To get to the trail from the playground, head south across the large, grassy field. Brown posts mark the beginning of the trail. Head east over the freeway and continue on. Barkley Village, Bellingham's newest shopping area, is about a twenty minute walk from the park.

PORT OF BELLINGHAM PARKS
These parks, run by the Port, are located on Bellingham Bay and are excellent places to watch sunsets.

Zuanich Point Park
Squalicum Harbor, Bellingham; 676-2500

Feature Highlights: kite flying, paved walking trail, picnicking, telescope
Driving Directions: Head west on Roeder Avenue. Turn left on Coho Way and then turn left again at the first street. Drive along the marina to the park's entrance.

Zuanich Point Park is a little tricky to find at first, but once you do, you'll go back again for the outstanding views of the San Juans, Bellingham Bay, and Mount Baker. A telescope is set up within the park so visitors may get a closer look at an object that catches their attention. Kite flying enthusiasts like to come here to launch their crafts, and kite tie-downs are provided for them. Visitors also enjoy walking, biking, or skating on the Harbor Promenade. This scenic 1.3 mile paved trail begins in the park and makes almost a complete loop around Squalicum Harbor.

View from Zuanich Point Park

Marine Park
West end of Harris Ave., Bellingham; 676-2500

Feature Highlights: beach access, picnicking, restrooms

This waterfront park near the Bellingham Cruise Terminal is a popular place to picnic and to watch sunsets. Many people like to get a to-go lunch or dinner in Fairhaven and enjoy it here.

Parks in
Whatcom County

These parks lie outside the city of Bellingham and are maintained by different agencies. We have three state parks in Whatcom County: Larrabee, Peace Arch, and Birch Bay. The rest of the parks are run by the cities in which they are located or by the Whatcom County Parks and Recreation Office. In considering all the parks in Whatcom County, including those in Bellingham, I would have to say that Hovander Homestead Park is my all time favorite. Its enormous red barn, farm animals, well tended farmhouse, and beautiful gardens make it a charming, serene place to visit.

The Whatcom County map on pages 6 and 7 shows the location of the major parks in this chapter.

Berthusen Park
8837 Berthusen Rd., Lynden; 354-2424

Feature Highlights: antique farm equipment, camping, homestead barn, old growth forest, picnicking, restrooms, trails
Driving Directions: From I-5 take the Birch Bay-Lynden Road exit (270) and head west 8 miles to Berthusen Road. Turn left. Park entrance is on the left in approximately 1.75 miles.

Hans C. Berthusen, an early pioneer settler, was a visionary. When he claimed a homestead near Lynden in the late 1800s, he set aside twenty acres of virgin timber as a reminder of what the country looked like when he arrived. Upon his death in 1944 he bequeathed his entire 236 acre homestead to the city of Lynden to be used as a memorial park. Thank you, Mr. Berthusen. Today visitors can view the old homestead barn and farm equipment, camp, picnic, or walk on paths that wind through old growth fir and cedar.

Birch Bay State Park
5105 Helweg Rd., Birch Bay; 371-2800 or 1-800-233-0321

Feature Highlights: beaches, bird watching, camping, clamming, picnicking, restrooms, trails
Driving Directions: From I-5 take the Grandview exit (266), head west, and follow the signs. The park is approximately 7 miles from I-5.

The draw of this park is the saltwater shoreline along Birch Bay. During the winter it's a wonderful spot to see Great Blue Herons, Bald Eagles, and other birds such as geese, loons, and scoters. If you can, try to come to this park during the summer. Wide expanses of beach are exposed and families like to dig for clams, explore tidepools, or wade in the warm water.

Be sure to check out the Terrell Marsh Trail located near the Registration Booth. This 1.5 mile loop trail takes you around Terrell Creek Marsh, one of the few remaining saltwater/freshwater estuaries in northern Puget Sound.

During the summer a trolley bus runs from Birch Bay State Park to the *Plover* ferry dock in Blaine. This scenic one hour loop costs fifty cents for adults and is free for children seven and younger. For more information about this year's trolley schedule, call Whatcom Transit Authority at 676-RIDE or 354-RIDE.

Blaine Marine Park
Marine Dr., Blaine; 332-8820

Feature Highlights: amphitheater, picnicking, sculptures, sunsets, trails, water views
Driving Directions: From Bellingham drive north on I-5 and take the Blaine City Center exit (276). Turn left under the freeway and then right on Marine Drive. The park is across the street from the Blaine Visitor's Center.

This seven acre park along Semiahmoo Bay is a great place to watch waterfowl in the winter and sunsets in the summer. Visitors can walk along the limestone paths within the park or on the quarter mile paved path that runs along Marine Drive. Kids enjoy climbing on the Orca whale sculptures or watching the water cascade down the salmon wall sculpture. During the summer this park makes a good place to picnic before or after you ride the *Plover*, a free foot passenger ferry that leaves from the Blaine Visitor's

29

Dock on weekends during the summer months. For more information about the *Plover* see page 107.

Hovander Homestead Park
5299 Nielsen Rd., Ferndale; 384-3444

Feature Highlights: enormous red barn, farm animals, gardens, playground, restrooms, tour of Hovander House (summers only), trails, water tower
Driving directions: From I-5 take the Ferndale City Center exit (262). Head west toward Ferndale. At the railroad underpass turn left and then turn right on Nielsen Road. Follow signs to the park's entrance.

Hovander is one of the most charming parks in Whatcom County. Its enormous red barn, handsome farmhouse, and immaculate lawns and gardens make it seem like you're visiting a well-to-do farming family. In a way, you are. The Hakan Hovander family, wealthy immigrants from Sweden, built the house in the early 1900s and lived there until 1971, when they turned over the ownership of the homestead to the Whatcom County Parks and Recreation Board. The restored Hovander House is open to the public during the summer. There is no entrance fee, but donations are accepted. Be sure to stop by the display gardens behind the house. These gardens are maintained by Master Gardeners from Whatcom County to educate visitors about soil preparation, composting, and weed identification.

A big draw for kids at Hovander is the assortment of farm animals near the barn. Horses, sheep, goats, pigs, fowl, and bunnies are housed in pens from spring to fall. A few animals, such as chickens, geese, ducks, and rabbits, winter over. Resident peacocks run free all year. Families also enjoy picnicking at Hovander. Its plentiful grassy areas with picnic tables and barbeques make it a popular place on summer weekends. The playground at Hovander features two swings, a wooden climbing structure with slides, and an old tractor on which to ride.

For a pleasant walk, families can stroll along the half mile trail to Tennant Lake Interpretive Center. This trail begins past the fowl pen, crosses a bridge, and continues on to Tennant Lake. See page 42 for what to do once you get there.

Barn at Hovander Homestead Park. Photo courtesy of Whatcom County Parks.

Larrabee State Park
245 Chuckanut Dr., Bellingham; 676-2093

Feature Highlights: beach combing, bicycling, boat launch, camping, clamming, hiking, picnicking, view points
Driving Directions: From I-5 take the Chuckanut Drive exit (205) and head west. At the first light turn left and drive 7 miles down Chuckanut Drive to the park's entrance.

Larrabee State Park holds the honor of being Washington's first state park. Families can find plenty to do within its 2,683 acres. One popular activity is to explore the rocky shoreline along Samish Bay. Starfish, mussels, crabs, and sea anemones can be found around the beach and tide pools. To get to the beach, park in the main parking lot south of the campground. Head left near the bandstand and follow the trail through a short tunnel and then down some stairs to the shore.

If your family likes to hike, Larrabee Park offers several different trails. The Interurban Trail is nearly six miles long and runs from Larrabee to the Fairhaven district in South Bellingham. This trail was once the roadbed for the interurban trolley that ran from Bellingham to Mount Vernon. Its nearly level grade makes it popular with hikers and bikers alike. To reach this trail, park at the trailhead to Fragrance Lake (across the road from the main park entrance) and hike up the path a short way until you come to the Interurban, a wide gravel trail. Head left to begin your walk. The two mile hike to Fragrance Lake is also popular. Cross the Interurban and continue up the trail. In nearly a mile you will come to a junction. Head left for a viewpoint of the San Juan Islands or right to continue hiking to Fragrance Lake. The hike to the viewpoint and back

View from the beach at Larrabee State Park

makes a pleasant family trip. It's short, not too steep, and scenic. The hike to Fragrance Lake, however, gets steep in places so it's best suited for older children. If you'd like a longer walk, you can take the loop trail around the lake before heading back.

On a clear day the 3.5 mile drive up Cleator Road, located north of the park entrance, is worth the trip. From the Cyrus Gates Overlook at the top, visitors have a breathtaking view of water and islands.

To reach the Larrabee Park boat launch, drive down Cove Road, which is located north of the park entrance.

Lighthouse Marine Park
811 Marine Dr., Point Roberts; 945-4911

Feature Highlights: boat launch, boardwalk, beaches, camping, fishing, picnic shelters, restrooms, trails, viewing tower, whale watching

Driving Directions: Take I-5 to the Peach Arch border crossing in Blaine. Once through customs, drive north 18 miles on Highway 99. Take the Highway 17 exit and head west for 5 miles. Take the Tsawwassen exit. Follow 56th Street to the Point Roberts border. Go through customs and follow the main road past the marina to the park.

When Britain and the U.S. were divvying territory back in 1846, both counties agreed that land south of the 49th parallel would belong to the United States. This seemed like a good idea. However, Point Roberts didn't fit neatly into this scheme. It is below the 49th parallel, but to drive to it, a person must enter Canada first. This extra hurdle prevents many Whatcom County residents from exploring Point Roberts. It's time to buck up that courage and head north. It took me an hour to drive to Lighthouse Marine Park from Bellingham. The border crossings went smoothly and there wasn't much traffic. I know this isn't always the case, though, and there can be long lines of cars at the border. When I reached Point Roberts, it seemed odd to be back in Whatcom County when I knew full well that I was still across the border. However, Whatcom County it was, and when I reached Lighthouse Marine Park, the familiar green and brown Whatcom County Parks sign made me feel at home. Once in Lighthouse Park, visitors can stroll along the half mile saltwater beach or along the gravel pathway that borders the beach. Picnic shelters and tables are available along the fifty-two thousand square feet of boardwalk. Nearby is a twenty foot viewing tower that children like to climb. When I was there the park was deserted, but manager Ben VanBuskirk said that on a sunny July weekend, people flock to the park to watch the resident Orca whales. Well! As it turns out, the San Juan Islands isn't the only place with resident Orcas. Whales from the J, K, and L pods swim by Point Roberts nearly everyday in July. They come to feast on the salmon. Why don't you come, too?

Lynden City Park
8460 Depot Rd., Lynden; 354-6717

Feature Highlights: Fishtrap Creek, paved trail, picnic shelter, playground, restrooms, tennis courts
Driving Directions: From Main Street in Lynden, head north on 3rd Street. The park entrance will be on your right in a few blocks.

I liked discovering this park one summer. The tall conifers make it a cool place to spend the afternoon on a warm day. Kids will enjoy poking around the shallow, rocky creek, playing at the playground, or walking through the open evergreen forest.

Peace Arch State Park
I-5 Border Crossing, Blaine; 332-8221

Feature Highlights: gardens, grassy areas, Peace Arch, picnic shelters, restrooms
Driving Directions: From I-5 take the Blaine City Center exit (274) and follow the signs.

Quick! How can you easily set foot in Canada without going through customs? By going to Peace Arch State Park. The big white monument that you see on the way to the Canadian Customs near Blaine really is on the border between the U.S. and Canada. Stroll north past the monument and *voila!* You're in Canada. Of course, if you want to formally visit, you must first go through Canadian Customs.

Peace Arch State Park and its Canadian sister park to the north, Provincial Park, were developed in 1920 to commemorate 100 years of an open, undefended boundary between the two countries. The Peach Arch itself was built with volunteer labor from the U.S. and Canada. Children from both of these countries donated money to complete the park areas around the arch. Today, many international celebrations are held in this park.

Visitors can enjoy the enormous grassy lawns, wander through the beautiful gardens, or learn more about the park and its monument by reading the informational displays.

Pioneer Park

1998 Cherry St., Ferndale; 384-3042

Feature Highlights: grassy areas, new playground, original pioneer log cabins (tours available in summer)
Driving Directions: From I-5 take the Ferndale City Center exit (262). Head west into Ferndale and watch for signs.

Pioneer Park, which was established in 1901, is a wonderful place to take the family. It has an outstanding collection of original pioneer log cabins arranged in a village setting. Only one cabin was originally built on site; the rest were moved in over the course of several years. The cabins are furnished with period artifacts and are open for tours mid-May through mid-September, Tuesday through Sunday, 11:30am to 4:30pm. Cost is $2 for adults and $1 for seniors and students. Children 10 and younger get in free. Even when these cabins are not open, it's fun to walk around them and imagine what it must have been like to live back in pioneer days.

General Store at Pioneer Park

37

Besides the cabins, Pioneer Park also has a large, new playground with equipment geared for children of all ages. Toddlers will enjoy climbing up and sliding down in Toddlertown—a piece of equipment especially scaled for them. Older kids will enjoy the swings and slides, the monkey bars, and the climbing equipment.

Samish Park
673 N. Lake Samish Dr., Bellingham; 733-2363

Feature Highlights: boat rentals (summer only), picnicking, playground, restrooms, sandy swimming beach, trails
Driving Directions: From I-5 take the North Lake Samish exit (246) and drive south on North Lake Samish Drive until you reach the park entrance.

This pretty park located on the north end of Lake Samish is a popular place to spend the afternoon on hot, summer days. Unfortunately, the parking lot fills quickly so either come early or be prepared to walk a long way. The

Sunbathers at Samish Park. Photo courtesy of Whatcom County Parks.

swimming area has a sandy beach and lifeguards are on duty from mid-June to Labor Day. Handsome picnic areas are available near the playground. This small playground has one baby and one regular swing, a climbing structure, and a slide. During the summer, non-motorized boats such as canoes and kayaks are available to rent. A drawback to this peaceful park is the noise from the power boats and jet skis that zip by during the warm weather.

Semiahmoo Park
9261 Semiahmoo Pkwy., Blaine; 733-2900

Feature Highlights: beach combing, bird watching, clamming, paved trail, water views
Driving Directions: From I-5 take the Birch Bay-Lynden Road exit (270), head west, and follow the signs. The park is 7 miles from I-5.

This narrow park runs along the sand spit at Semiahmoo. Families can walk along the 0.8 mile paved path or on the beach. This is a good place to spot Great Blue Herons wading in the water. Views from the spit include Mt. Baker, Drayton Harbor, and the marina at Semiahmoo. The city of White Rock, British Columbia, is spread out on the hill across the bay. When you reach the end of the paved trail, you can either turn around, poke around the Inn at Semiahmoo, an upscale resort, or walk among the boats at the marina. The nearby Mercantile store caters to boaters and sells groceries and other boat related items. Bicycles are also available to rent there.

In the summer, families can catch the *Plover*, a restored foot passenger ferry, from the dock behind the Inn at Semiahmoo. This free boat takes you to Blaine Harbor and back. The round trip lasts about fifty minutes. For more information about the *Plover* see page 107.

Silver Lake Park
9006 Silver Lake Rd., Sumas; 599-2776

Feature Highlights: boat launch, boat rentals (summer only), cabin rentals, camping, day lodge, fishing, food concession (summers only), historical house, picnicking, play area, restrooms, trails

Driving directions: From I-5 take Mt. Baker Highway exit (255) and drive east 28 miles to Maple Falls. Turn left on Silver Lake Road. The park entrance will be on your right in approximately 3 miles.

B oating, fishing, hiking, and picnicking are all popular activities within this park's 411 acres. During the summer, visitors can rent non-motorized boats, such as canoes, rowboats, or pedal boats, to explore the lake. If you already own your own boat, a public boat launch is provided. To rent boats, inquire at the day lodge. Inside the lodge, visitors will also find a tackle shop, a seasonal food concession area, and more information about the park. Along the lake, families will find a children's play area, picnic tables, and beaches. Hiking trails run through the park.

Silver Lake Park was a resort before Whatcom County Parks purchased it in 1969. Some of the original cabins still remain and are available to rent year around. Across the road from the park entrance, visitors can see the historical Gerdrum House. This house, built in 1892 from the lumber from one cedar log, was the area's first home. It's currently boarded up, but plans are in the works to re-open it to the public.

Squires Lake Park
Trailhead located on Highway 99 between I-5 South Lake Samish and Alger exits; 384-3444

Feature Highlights: beaver pond, hiking trails
Driving Directions: From Bellingham take I-5 south to the Nulle Road exit (242). Turn left under the freeway and then follow the road to the right. The parking lot will be on your left in approximately one half mile.

Squires Lake Park, Whatcom County's newest park, is a place where families can hike through conifers and deciduous trees to a lake and a beaver pond. The lake is about a fifteen minute hike from the trailhead. Even though the trail heads uphill, our four year old made it just fine. On the day we were there, the water was perfectly calm and the reflections in it were marvelous. Families may turn around here or continue on to the beaver pond. At the pond we didn't see any beavers, but we did see one of their dams. The sticks that make up these dams have neat rows of teeth marks all along them where beavers have gnawed off the bark. Some were scattered on the ground near the pond, so we got to examine them closely. The sticks were a hit with our kids. We also spotted stumps with teeth marks in them where beavers had chomped down trees. This was a good winter hike with kids—short, scenic, and not too muddy.

Tennant Lake Interpretive Center
5236 Nielson Rd., Ferndale; 384-3444

Feature Highlights: boardwalk trail, Environmental Interpretive Center, Fragrance Gardens, restrooms, Tennant Lake
Hours for Interpretive Center: Thursday-Saturday 12pm-4pm
Driving Directions: From I-5 take the Ferndale City Center exit (262) and head west into Ferndale. Turn left under the railroad overpass and then make a right on Nielsen Road. Follow the signs to the park.

The big farmhouse you see when you drive into this park was built in 1906 for the C. M. Nielsen family. Whatcom County Parks and Recreation Board bought it from them in 1975 and converted it into an environmental interpretive center for the area around Tennant Lake. Funding for the interpretive center is sketchy, so the house isn't always open. It's best to call ahead to make sure. However, most families come to Tennant Lake to enjoy the gardens and to hike along the boardwalk trail.

The Fragrance Garden, located next to the Nielsen house, was designed for the non-sighted, but everyone enjoys it. Raised beds put fragrant plants right at nose level. Take a deep breath and inhale the scent of Chocolate Cosmos, peppermint, or lavender. The paths through the garden are wide enough to accommodate wheelchairs. Signs are in Braille and in print.

The trail to the boardwalk begins behind the Fragrance Gardens. Walk along the gravel path and over a bridge until you come to the actual boardwalk. This 1.4 mile loop trail zigzags through the marshy area around the lake and is a good place to see Red-winged Blackbirds, aquatic birds, and the occasional muskrat. Whatcom County Parks and Recreation bought Tennant Lake in conjunction with the Department of Fish and Wildlife, so the boardwalk trail closes during hunting season, usually the second Sunday in October to the second Sunday in January. A sign near the beginning of the trail alerts visitors to boardwalk closure dates.

Tennant Lake Interpretive Center

Whatcom Museum of

History and Art

Museums

Whatcom County's museums are as diverse as its citizens. From the highly regarded Whatcom Museum of History and Art to the hands-on science activities at Mindport, families will find exhibits that appeal to a variety of interests.

Bellingham Antique Radio Museum

1315 Railroad Ave., Bellingham; 671-4663

Hours: Wednesday-Sunday 12pm-5pm
Cost: Free

M y brother-in-law once remarked to me, after visiting Bellingham, that this city seems to be full of collectors. "How so?" I inquired. "Just think of the Antique Radio Museum," he began. I did. It's true. Bellingham is home to some outstanding collections, and Jonathan Winter's collection of early radios and associated technology is among them. His museum on Railroad Avenue is chock-a-block full of items he has gathered over his lifetime. This early technology was definitely hands-on, and kids are encouraged to turn knobs, push buttons, and pull levers. Winter has one of the earliest phonographs designed by Thomas Edison. Visitors can record their voices onto a wax cylinder and then play it back. You'll discover quite a contrast between this sound and the sound we hear from our CDs today.

Display outside the Bellingham Antique Radio Museum

Plans are in the works to move this museum to a larger space and to expand its educational outreach program. In the meantime, head on down, enjoy the collection, and pepper Jonathan Winter or his assistant curator, Paul Niederhour, with questions. Their passion for this early technology is contagious.

Lynden Pioneer Museum
217 W. Front St., Lynden; 354-3675

Hours: Monday-Saturday 10am-4pm. Closed Sunday.
Cost: Adults $3; Youth (14 and under) Free; Seniors and students $2

The Lynden Pioneer Museum is a real treasure in Whatcom County. It should be on every family's "Let's Check This Out" list. The museum began in 1976 when Fred Polinder, a local resident in his 90s, bequeathed his large collection of buggies, wagons, and carriages to the City of Lynden with the stipulation that they be on display. Well, they are on display along with thousands of other objects that help visitors understand what life has been like in Whatcom County over the past 100 years. The Polinder collection has been augmented over the years, and there's now a wonderful and vast assortment of old tractors, cars, buggies, and bicycles. The vehicle collection is worth seeing even if you don't consider yourself a vehicle buff. Besides the vehicle collection, another highlight is the replica of Front Street in Lynden as it was in the 1920s and 30s. The buildings are on two levels and include twenty-six shops and businesses. Visitors to the museum can also learn about the history of Lynden and its local industries, such as dairy farming and logging.

Mindport

111 Grand Ave., Bellingham; 647-5614

Hours: Wednesday-Sunday, 10am-5pm. Closed Monday and Tuesday.
Cost: Free

If you haven't been to Mindport yet, you need to go soon. This hands-on discovery museum is as exciting for preschoolers as it is for grandparents. The exhibits are ingeniously designed from common objects. One exhibit consists of a large, upright felt board, white plastic pipe, elbow joints, and miniature balls. The piping, some cut in half lengthwise, some left whole, has velcro glued on it. The piping sticks to the felt board. Kids (and grownups, too!) can spend a lot of time constructing different paths for the balls to traverse. Another exhibit, fashioned out of plexiglass and plywood, uses odd bits of styrofoam and

Young explorer at Mindport

stuffed animals to help visitors explore the properties of static electricity. Live plants, photographs of sea creatures, and mobiles made of driftwood and leaves complement the exhibits. This creative, thoughtful museum is made possible by an anonymous Whatcom County benefactor. We are lucky indeed.

WHATCOM MUSEUM CAMPUS

The Whatcom Museum Campus is composed of four buildings along Prospect Street: The Whatcom Museum of History and Art, the Arco Exhibits Building, the Syre Education Center, and the Whatcom Children's Museum. The first three are **open Tuesday through Sunday, 12pm to 5pm,** and are closed Monday. Admission is free, but donations are encouraged. The Children's Museum has different hours and charges admission.

Whatcom Museum of History and Art
121 Prospect St., Bellingham; 676-6981

This beautiful red brick building trimmed with Chuckanut sandstone was built in 1892 as a city hall. While the outside remains essentially unchanged, the inside has been remodeled to accommodate its current function as a museum. Its first and second floors are used for changing history and art exhibits. The third floor houses examples of Victorian clothing and toys, woodworking tools, and clock works.

Behind the museum a hill climb was recently completed. This wide set of concrete stairs leads people down to Maritime Heritage Center (see page 17) and offers wonderful views of Bellingham Bay and Old Town.

Arco Exhibits Building
206 Prospect St., Bellingham; 676-6981

This museum's changing art and history exhibits sometimes feature hands-on shows that especially appeal to kids, like a recent exhibit on mechanical banks. Visitors could drop pennies into the slots on the banks and watch them move in comical ways.

Syre Education Center
201 Prospect St., Bellingham; 676-6981

If you've ever wondered what the names of those little brown birds are in your backyard, or if you've ever wanted to show your child a Pileated Woodpecker up close, then the Syre Education Center is a good place to come. It houses a wonderful collection of over 200 birds found in Washington State. The stuffed birds are grouped by families (raptors, perchers, aquatic birds, etc.) and identification guides are available. This museum also houses Victorian era period rooms, Northwest Coast First Nations and Inuit exhibits, First Nations baskets, and Logging and Settlement exhibits.

Whatcom Children's Museum
227 Prospect St., Bellingham; 733-8769

Hours: Sunday/ Tuesday/ Wednesday 12pm-5pm; Thursday-Saturday 10am-5pm. Closed Monday.
Cost: $2/person

This interactive, hands-on museum is designed for children eight and younger, although the bulk of its visitors seem to be preschoolers and kindergartners. The Children's Museum provides extensive opportunities for children to keep their minds and bodies actively engaged. Every six to nine months or so, the exhibits change. During a recent exhibit children learned about money by panning for "gold," manipulating a giant abacus, or viewing money from around the world. This exhibit complemented the exhibit on mechanical banks which was shown at the Arco Building across the street.

Even though some exhibits change, some remain the same. The Discovery Center is a place where children can browse through books, watch small animals in aquariums, or put together intriguing puzzles. In the Learning Center, children can make simple art projects—materials and directions are provided—or create their own. Wonder Boxes

Puppet Playhouse at the Children's Museum

are also available for parents and children to check out together. These plastic tubs contain interesting items which relate to different themes such as music, literature, or science.

Every Friday and Saturday the museum holds workshops for children. These workshops are held in the Learning Center and vary each week. For example, children may learn about groundhogs, celebrate Switzerland, or act out classic stories with handmade puppets. Preschool Treasure Chest is held on Fridays from 10:30am to 11:30am. This workshop is free with the price of admission and is geared for children three to six years old. Wonder Workshops are held on Saturdays from 1pm to 3pm and are appropriate for school age children. Costs vary with the program.

Animals

K ids love to watch animals, whether they're viewed on a farm, in a pet store, or in the wild. For the animal lovers in your family, try one of the following places.

Bellingham Trout Hatchery
1700 Silver Beach Rd., Bellingham; 676-2138

Hours: Everyday 8am-5pm

This hatchery, located in Whatcom Falls Park, raises trout to stock area lakes and streams. Visitors can watch the small trout swimming in their rearing pens and learn more about the fish hatchery by reading the informational displays. For more information on other activities in Whatcom Falls Park, see page 18.

Hovander Homestead Park
5299 Nielsen Rd., Ferndale; 384-3444

Children love to come to Hovander to see the assortment of farm animals near the barn. Horses, sheep, goats, pigs, fowl, and bunnies are housed in pens from spring to fall. A few animals such as chickens, geese, ducks, and rabbits winter over. Resident peacocks run free all year. For more information about other activities at this park, see page 30.

Geese are year round residents at Hovander Park.

54

Marine Life Center
1801 Roeder Ave., Bellingham; 671-2431

Hours: Everyday 8am-dusk
Cost: Free

This small, well-kept exhibit lets visitors view local marine life up close. Children love to stand around the observation pool and watch fish swim around sea stars, urchins, sea cucumbers, and starry flounders. Nearby is a touch pool full of sea anemones, sea stars, shells, and different kinds of crabs. Children may gently touch or pick up these creatures. Towels are handily located nearby so kids can dry their hands after exploring. Visitors can also learn about marine life by reading the informational posters or by observing the creatures in three different aquariums.

PET STORES
Each of Whatcom County's four main pet stores offers something a little different. I would like to thank pet store owners for allowing children to come in and just look. Our family makes weekly trips to Hohl's and Clark's.

Hohl Feed & Seed
1322 Railroad Ave., Bellingham; 734-0300

Hours: Monday-Saturday 9am-6pm. Closed Sunday.

The nice feature about Hohl's is that kids can get close to the animals. Cages of mice, guinea pigs, rats, and hamsters are at eye level. The kitty cage is right there, too, so kids can reach their fingers in to pet the soft fur. Bunnies are often for sale. Don't miss the bird and fish rooms in the back of the store.

Clark Feed & Seed

1326 Railroad Ave., Bellingham; 733-8330

Hours: Monday-Saturday 9am-6pm. Closed Sunday.

If you've ever wanted to set up a fresh or saltwater aquarium, Clark's is the place to come. They carry hundreds of different kinds of fish, plus all the supplies to keep them happy. Kitties are often for sale here, too.

Sunset Pets

Sunset Square; 1225 E. Sunset Dr., Bellingham; 647-7818

Hours: Monday-Saturday 10am-7pm; Sunday 11am-6pm

At Sunset Pets kids can see a wide variety of fish, reptiles, and amphibians. A cage full of crickets is here, too. They also carry kittens, puppies, bunnies, and birds. These animals are kept in cages behind glass walls, so you can look at them, but not touch them.

Petsmart

4379 Meridian, Bellingham; 738-9653

Hours: Monday-Saturday 9am-8pm; Sunday 9am-6pm

This large store near Costco on Meridian carries a variety of reptiles (no snakes), rodents, birds, and over 100 aquariums full of fish.

Sardis Wildlife Center
7472 Valley View Rd., Ferndale; 366-3863

Hours: Open to the public Wednesday and Saturday from 11am to 4pm
Cost: Free
Driving Directions: From I-5 take the Grandview exit (266) and head west for 3 miles. Turn right on Valley View Road and drive 1.4 miles. The entrance to the center will be on your right. Follow the road a short distance through the woods. The visitor parking lot is just beyond the one designated for volunteers.

When you step out of your car at Sardis, you will probably be greeted by one of the friendly, resident cats and be looked upon with curiosity by the band of roving peacocks. The dogs behind the gate at the caretaker's house will bark and wag their tails. When it's quiet you can hear the calls of different raptors. Welcome to the world of animals.

Sardis Wildlife Center has been in Whatcom County since 1989. Its purpose is to rehabilitate injured animals and then release them back into the wild. Since 1995 Sardis has concentrated on birds of prey and has become one of the largest raptor facilities in the Northwest. It's open to the public two days a week. Visitors can see eagles, hawks, owls, and falcons. The birds on display are housed in large cages outside. They have been past patients at Sardis, but their injuries prevented them from being released; a one-eyed owl doesn't last very long in nature. While my son is the bird lover in our family, we were all thrilled to see an American Kestral, Peregrine Falcon, Snowy Owl, and several Bald Eagles up close.

When you go, don't expect posh facilities and tour guides. While the center is tidy and well kept, it's also run on a shoestring budget. You're pretty much on your own to walk around and look at the animals. If you'd like a tour of the facility, including the hospital, x-ray, and surgery areas, please call the center to make reservations. The tour lasts about an hour and a half and costs $2/person.

Viewing a raptor at Sardis Wildlife Center

Wild Bird Crossing
Sunset Square, Bellingham; 738-7088

Hours: Monday-Saturday 10am-6pm; Sunday 12pm-5pm

While the Wild Bird Crossing doesn't carry any actual live birds, they do carry all the necessary equipment for feeding and attracting wild birds to your back yard. Our family bought a bird feeder this year, and now each member can identify the house finches, chickadees, nuthatches, and sparrows that visit frequently. This store also carries a wide selection of books, audio and video tapes, and spotting scopes. A table with crayons and paper is thoughtfully set up near the book department so children may color while their parents browse.

Indoor Activities

If the Northwest rains have hit, whether it's January or June, try one of the following indoor activities to help your child expend some of that kid energy.

Arne Hannah Aquatic Center
1114 Potter St., Bellingham; 647-7665

Hours: Monday-Friday 5:30am-10pm; Saturday 8:30am-10pm; Sunday 8:30am-10pm
Cost: Youth (17 and under) $2.50; Adult (18 and over) $3.50; Senior (62 and over) $2

The Bellingham Aquatic Center opened in 1995. The handsome brick building houses four pools—a lap pool, a wading pool, a dive tank, and a hydrotherapy pool. It also has a 135 foot waterslide in the shape of a tube that travels outside before it comes back in again. Children must be at least four feet tall to use the waterslide.

Different pools are open at different times of the day, so it's a good idea to call ahead to make sure the pool you want to use is available. Family Swim, which is usually held Monday through Friday from 12:30pm-2:30pm, is a time when all four pools, but not the waterslide, are open. Entrance fees are half off during this family swim. On Friday there's a Preschool Swim which is especially designed for preschoolers and their families. Swim diapers are not mandatory on young children who aren't toilet trained yet. They may wear either cloth or disposable diapers as long as the diaper is covered by plastic pants with elastic around the leg holes and waist.

The Aquatic Center has changing rooms for men and women, plus two family changing rooms. The family changing rooms are private and are designed for parents to use with their children seven years old and younger. The rooms come equipped with hand held showers, benches, and baby changing tables. Children over seven years old should use the changing room that's appropriate for their gender.

Safety lessons at the Aquatic Center. Photo courtesy of the Aquatic Center.

Bellingham Cruise Terminal

335 Harris Ave., Bellingham; 650-2500

Hours: Monday-Thursday 8am-5pm; Friday 8am-6pm; Saturday & Sunday 10am-5pm

From the outside, the Cruise Terminal looks handsome and stately with its red bricks and arched windows. From the inside, visitors are treated to one of the best water views in Bellingham. On rainy or cold days buy a cup of hot chocolate from Barnacles, the small cafe inside the terminal, sit at one of the tables in the glassed in rotunda, and enjoy the view. From your seat you can watch seagulls swooping over fishing boats, see the Alaska ferry come in on Friday mornings or depart Friday afternoons, or look straight across Bellingham Bay and view Squalicum Harbor and, on clear days, the Canadian Coast Range.

Besides being able to enjoy stupendous views, the terminal is also a great place to take your toddler during inclement weather. Its wide-open spaces, lack of crowds, and two levels make it an ideal place to walk around with an active child. You can walk up and down the stairs, make several loops around the second floor, and watch the waterfront activity from the many picture windows.

The following shop and restaurant are located inside the terminal and are open every day.

Inside Passage
734-1790
Hours: Every day 10am-5pm

This small gift shop sells items with a Northwest flavor. Visitors can purchase stuffed animals, tee shirts, jewelry, food items, mugs, and books.

Barnacles
647-5072

Hours: Monday-Friday 8am-5pm; Saturday & Sunday 10am-5pm (Sunday 4pm)

In the morning Barnacles serves breakfast items such as eggs, pancakes, cinnamon rolls, or bagels. For lunch or dinner you can order salads, sandwiches, hamburgers, or seafood such as clam chowder or halibut and chips.

Kindergym

Multipurpose Room; Bloedel Donovan Park, Bellingham;
676-6985

Hours: Monday/Wednesday/Friday 10am-11:30am
Cost: $2/child per visit

Kindergym is a good place to meet other parents and allow your preschooler to work off some energy. The gym at Bloedel Donovan Park is open three days a week for an hour and a half and is set up with kid-friendly activities. Your child can tumble on mats, shoot some hoops, balance on a beam, or toss bean bags. Although an instructor is on duty, parents are expected to supervise their children. During part of the time at Kindergym, the instructor leads activities such as parachute games or using rhythm sticks to tap out beats.

Shooting a basket at Kindergym

63

Kindergym is set up on a timecard system. This means that parents need to purchase a timecard on their first visit. Cards are valid for two months and are kept at the gym. Parents can choose which days to attend. The program is set up on a drop-in basis. Fees are based on $2 per child per visit. Let's say you had one child and you figured you'd come to Kindergym once a week for the next two months. Your cost would be $16—eight visits at $2 per visit. Kindergym has space available for forty participants. On the day we went, Kindergym had sold out their available spaces. We were allowed to participate for free that day and then our name was put on a waiting list. It took six weeks to get called back. If you think you would be interested in attending Kindergym on a regular basis, I suggest you call to see when the best time is to sign up.

Lynden Skateway
421 Judson St., Lynden; 354-3851

Hours for public skating: Wednesday 6:30pm-9pm; Friday 7pm-11pm; Saturday 1pm-4pm and 7pm-11pm; Sunday 1pm-4pm and 6:30pm-9pm
Cost: Prices vary from $3 to $5.50 depending on your age and the time of day you skate. Price includes skate rentals.

Whatcom County residents were glad when the Lynden Skateway re-opened in 1996. Two years earlier a fire had destroyed the original Skateway, which was the only indoor roller rink around. Now it's open again, it's new, and it's fun! The Lynden Skateway is a family oriented place, and you can be assured of a wholesome atmosphere when you go. Signs with dress and conduct codes are prominently displayed at the entrance. A concession stand is open for an energy boost after all that exercise.

Play Area at Bellis Fair Mall
I-5 and Meridian; Located in the Target Wing

Hours: Monday-Saturday 10am-9pm; Sunday 11am-6pm
Cost: Free

On rainy days when your kids need to get their ya-ya's out, the play area at Bellis Fair Mall is a good place to come. It's located near Target and is situated under a large, domed skylight. Inside the carpeted area are durable rubber objects in the shape of food. Your child can scramble on stacks of enormous cookies, climb on an oversized carton of orange juice, or jump on a huge peanutbutter and jelly sandwich.

ROCK CLIMBING WALLS
Indoor rock climbing has become popular recently, and Whatcom County has two main walls.

Leading Edge
Haskell Business Center
1409 Fraser St., Suite G, Bellingham; 733-6969

Hours: Monday-Thursday 5:30pm-9:30pm; Friday & Saturday 5:30pm-10:30pm; Sunday 2pm-7pm. The Saturday and Sunday hours begin in October.
Cost: Daily climbing $5; Rental package $3. Climbing passes are available.

Once inside, you'll realize Leading Edge also trains gymnasts. Mats and beams are everywhere. Their rock wall has areas both for beginners and for those with advanced skills. A trained climbing instructor is on duty at all times to assist those who need help.

65

Whatcom Family YMCA

1256 N. State St., Bellingham; 733-8630

Open Climb Times: Monday 10am-1pm and 6pm-10pm; Tuesday 7pm-10pm; Wednesday-Friday 6pm-10pm
Teen Climb Time: Tuesday & Thursday 3pm-5pm
Cost: Free for YMCA members; Non-member adults $5; Non-member youth (high school age and under) $3. Price includes harness and gri-gri belay device.

Certified climbing instructors are on hand during open and teen climb times to give participants assistance if they need it. Teens don't need to be accompanied by an adult during Teen Time Climb, but a parent/guardian signed waiver must be on file in the office. The non-member climbing fee actually buys participants a day pass to the YMCA, so after climbing, they may use any other of the facilities at the Y such as the pool, gym, or weight room.

Sport Zone

1788 Midway Ln., Bellingham; 734-4189

Hours: Monday-Thursday 11am-9pm; Friday 11am-11pm; Saturday 10am-10pm; Sunday 12pm-6pm

Sport Zone provides an opportunity for baseball players, basketball players, and golfers to practice their skills indoors. Three batting cages are set up and customers can choose to hit baseballs or softballs pitched at varying speeds. One round of eighteen pitches costs $1.25. Sport Zone also has two indoor basketball courts available to individuals or groups. Individuals pay $2 for thirty minutes of shooting or $3.50 for sixty minutes. Groups can rent the court for $12 for thirty minutes or $20 for sixty. Golfers can use the indoor driving range for $5 for fifteen minutes or $8 for thirty minutes. Sport Zone opened in September of 1998 and is becoming popular with local athletes who want to get a head start on their season.

Sportsplex
1225 Civic Field Way, Bellingham; 733-9999

Hours: Whatcom Community Skate Monday-Thursday 2:30-4pm. Public Skate Friday 6:30pm-10pm; Saturday 1pm-4:30pm and then from 6:30pm-10pm; Sunday 1pm-4:30pm.
Cost: Whatcom Community Skate $1/person, plus $2 skate rental. Public Skate $5/adults, $3.50/children (12 years old and younger), plus $2 skate rental.

The Sportsplex ice arena opened in 1997 and has been popular ever since. Be sure to dress warmly when you go. Yes, it's cold on the ice, but also in the building. A concession stand is available for snacks and hot beverages when you need to refuel.

Toddler Time
Multipurpose Room; Bloedel Donovan Park; 676-6985

Hours: Tuesday & Thursday 10am-11:30am

This free activity for parents and their children, ages three and under, is sponsored by the Bellingham Parks and Recreation Office. Bring your toddler's favorite ride-on toy from home and let her zoom around the gym while you get a chance to chat with other parents. Complimentary coffee and tea are provided. Some Toddler Time dates get cancelled, so call ahead or pick up a schedule when you go.

Tube Time
1522 Cornwall Ave., Bellingham; 715-9167

Hours: Monday-Saturday 10am-9pm; Sunday 11am-7pm
Cost (Monday-Thursday): Adults Free; Children (3 years and up) $4.95; Toddlers (2 years and under) $2.95. Every Tuesday is two for one day. Two children get in for the price of one.
Cost (Friday-Sunday): Adults Free; Children $5.45; Toddlers $3.45

Tube Time is an old Safeway grocery store that's been converted into a kid's idea of fun. The largest section is a huge jungle gym of tubes, ramps, and slides where kids can expend some of their abundant energy. Another section is full of arcade games and a third section is a play area for toddlers. In the center of all this action is a concession area with tables and chairs where parents can sit and swivel their heads from the tubes, to the arcade games, to the toddler area to make sure their progeny are happy. We like to go during the week right when Tube Time opens. It's pretty quiet then and we sometimes have the place to ourselves.

YMCAs

The YMCAs in Bellingham and in Lynden are open every day and sell day passes to non-members. The climbing wall at the Whatcom Family YMCA is a popular spot with kids.

Whatcom Family YMCA
1256 N. State St., Bellingham; 733-8630

Hours: Monday-Friday 5:30am-10pm; Saturday 6:30am-7pm; Sunday 12pm-7pm
Cost: Day pass $5/adults and $3/youth (high school age and under)

If you're not a member of the YMCA, you can buy a day pass to use any of the Y's facilities such as the climbing wall, gym, racketball courts, or weight room. The Y also has two pools. One is small and shallow and is good for young children; the other is large and is used for lap swims and open swims. At scheduled times the large pool is converted into a wave pool! Different facilities at the Y are open at different times of the day. Pick up a schedule or call ahead to find out when the facility you want to use is open.

Lynden YMCA Activity Center
100 Drayton St., Lynden; 354-5000

Hours: Monday-Thursday 5:30am-9:30pm; Friday 5:30am-10pm; Saturday 9am-10pm; Sunday 1pm-4pm
Cost: Day pass $5/adults and $3/youth (high school age and under)

The YMCA at Lynden has one large pool, a weight room, a gym, and racketball courts. Its facilities are also open for general use during different times of the day so be sure to pick up a schedule or to call ahead to make sure the facility you want to use is open.

Enjoying the wave pool at the Bellingham YMCA. Photo courtesy of the Bellingham YMCA.

Outdoor Activities

It's true that a bit of rain doesn't slow down most Whatcom County families. We like to be outside and are lucky to have an abundance of parks, trails, and waterways to explore. We can ski, swim, bicycle, or boat with our children.

If summer vacation is just around the corner, or it's winter break and you're looking for ideas of how to keep the troops occupied, try some of the following ideas.

BICYCLING

B icycling is a favorite past time for families in Whatcom County. It's no wonder. Our many trails provide a safe place on which to ride. The Interurban, a 5.9 mile trail from the Fairhaven District in Bellingham to Larrabee State Park, is one of the most popular. For a list of biking trails please read the information in the Favorite Walks section of this chapter. The trails listed there, with the exception of the Tennant Lake Boardwalk Trail, are multiple use trails, and families can hike or bike along them.

The following places rent bicycles in Whatcom County.

Fairhaven Bike and Mountain Sports
1103 11ᵗʰ St., Bellingham; 733-4433

Hours: Monday-Thursday 9:30am-7pm; Friday 9:30am-8pm; Saturday 10am-6pm; Sunday 11am-5pm

I f you've seen other bicyclists towing those bright yellow kid trailers behind them and would like to try one out, come to Fairhaven Bike. They rent these and trail-a-bikes, too. Trail-a-bikes attach to the rear of an adult's bike, making a hybrid tandem that works beautifully. We rented one to try with our four year old and wound up buying one. Now my daughter and I can zip to our local park or ride the many trails around Bellingham. Fairhaven Bike also rents road bikes and mountain bikes for kids or grownups.

Jack's Bicycle Center
1907 Iowa St., Bellingham; 733-1955

Hours: Monday-Friday 9:30am-5:30pm; Saturday 9:30am-4pm

Mountain bikes for adults are available to rent.

Semiahmoo Mercantile
9540 Semiahmoo Pkwy., Blaine; 371-5700

Hours: Monday-Friday 8:30am-5pm; Friday & Saturday 8:30am-6pm; Sunday 8:30am-5pm. Call for extended summer hours.

Customers can rent bikes and pedal along the paved trail in nearby Semiahmoo Park.

Bicyclers along the Interurban Trail

73

BOATING

Since Whatcom County is blessed with an abundance of lakes, rivers, and bays, boating is a popular family activity. Many of the area's parks rent boats during the summer and also have boat launches available. The following is a list of boat rentals and launches available in Whatcom County.

Blaine Harbor
Marine Dr., Blaine; 676-2500
Boat rentals: No
Boat launch: Yes

Bloedel Donovan Park
2214 Electric Ave., Bellingham; 676-6985
Boat rentals (seasonal): Lake kayaks, canoes, and pedal boats
Boat launch: Yes

Fairhaven Boatworks Inc.
510 Harris, Bellingham; 647-2469
Boat rentals (all year): Kayaks, rowboats, small and medium sailboats
Boat launch: Yes

Lake Padden Park
4882 Samish Wy., Bellingham; 676-6985
Boat rentals (seasonal): Lake kayaks and canoes
Boat launch: Yes

Larrabee State Park
245 Chuckanut Dr., Bellingham; 676-2093
Boat rentals: No
Boat launch: Yes

Lighthouse Marine Park
811 Marine Dr., Point Roberts; 945-4911
Boat rentals: Sometimes kayaks are available. Call to confirm
Boat launch: Yes

Samish Park
673 N. Lake Samish Dr., Bellingham; 733-2362 or 733-2900
Boat rentals (seasonal): Lake kayaks, canoes, and pedal boats
Boat launch: No

Silver Lake Park
9006 Silver Lake Rd., Sumas; 599-2776 or 733-2900
Boat rentals: Lake kayaks, canoes, and pedal boats
Boat launch: Yes

Squalicum Harbor
Roeder Ave., Bellingham; 676-2500
Boat rentals: No
Boat launch: Yes

FAVORITE WALKS

Whatcom County has many miles of trails that are suitable for families. The walks listed here are some of the most popular. For a comprehensive list of walks and hikes in our area, check out Ken Wilcox's excellent book, *Hiking Whatcom County*. It's available in area book stores.

Lake Padden Loop

This 2.8 mile loop around Lake Padden is one of the most popular walks in Whatcom County. The length is just about right for a decent workout and the scenery is tranquil. The section of trail along the lake is flat, and the part that travels through the woods contains a few hills. Jogging strollers work well on this loop.

Interurban Trail

This trail used to be the route that the Interurban Trolley took from Bellingham to Mt. Vernon. The tracks have long since been ripped up and now it's a well-maintained 5.9 mile trail from Fairhaven to Larrabee State Park. It makes a wonderful walking and biking trail since its grade is mostly level. The trailhead in Fairhaven is located off Old Fairhaven Parkway near 20th Street. The trail begins behind the parking lot. Walk along the gravel path and up a short hill until you come to the sidewalk. Turn left and continue down the sidewalk for half a block. Cross 20th Street and pick up the gravel trail again. Before you continue, you might want to stop at the nearby nursery, The Gardens at Padden Creek. It is open from March to September and has a wonderful selection of plants to peruse and a pen full of chickens and roosters to watch. If you continue past the nursery for another mile and a half you will come to a good place to turn around. Here stairs lead down to Old Samish Highway and Arroyo Park. If you want to continue on, go down the stairs, cross the road, and pick up the trail in Arroyo Park. This trail will cross a bridge and then go up a steep hill until it levels out again. It will remain mostly flat until it reaches Larrabee State Park.

Boulevard Park

The trail along the water's edge is a great place to watch boats, birds, and sunsets. Across Bellingham Bay you can see Lummi Island to the west, the port of Bellingham and the marina to the north, and the ferry terminal in Fairhaven to the south. If you would like to walk into downtown Bellingham from this park, cross the railroad tracks at the north end of the park and turn left onto the wide gravel trail. You will reach a pedestrian bridge in approximately one mile. Cross the trestle and go left by the brown posts. The trail comes out onto E. Maple Street near Railroad Avenue. To walk into Fairhaven from Boulevard Park, climb the stairs at the south end of the park, cross the railroad tracks, and walk up a gravel path. At 10th Street head south for two blocks and pick up the trail again. This trail comes out in Fairhaven at 10th and Mill Street. It's about a mile from the park into Fairhaven.

Tennant Lake Boardwalk Trail

This 1.4 mile loop trail zigzags through the marshy area around Tennant Lake and is a good place to see Red-winged Blackbirds, aquatic birds, and the occasional musk-rat. The trail begins behind the Fragrance Gardens at Tennant Lake Interpretive Center. Walk along the gravel

77

path and over a bridge until you come to the actual boardwalk part of the trail. Unfortunately for walkers, this trail
is closed for three months, beginning in early October.
Whatcom County Parks and Recreation bought Tennant
Lake in conjunction with the Department of Fish and Wildlife, so the boardwalk trail closes during hunting season.
A sign near the beginning of the trail alerts visitors to boardwalk closure dates.

Boardwalk trail at Tennant Lake

Semiahmoo Spit Trail

This 0.8 mile trail begins across the street from the parking lot at Semiahmoo Park in Blaine. The paved trail travels along Semiahmoo Spit and is a good place to see Great Blue Herons and other aquatic birds. On clear days visitors also have spectacular views of Mount Baker and the Canadian Coast Range. At the end of the trail you will come out at The Inn at Semiahmoo, an up-scale resort. The Mercantile store near the marina rents bikes and has snacks for sale.

Railroad Trail

Families can walk this 3.5 mile gravel trail from Bloedel Donovan Park to Sunnyland Memorial Park. It's fun to begin at Sunnyland, play at the playground for a while, and then walk on the trail mid-way to Barkley Village for a snack. This walk takes about fifteen minutes, one way. To access the trail from the playground, head south across the big, grassy field. Brown posts mark the beginning of the trail. To begin the trail at Bloedel Donovan, park at the trailhead across the street from the main parking lot.

Harbor Promenade

This 1.3 mile paved trail begins at Zuanich Point Park and makes almost a complete loop around Squalicum Harbor. Families enjoy walking, skating or biking on this scenic trail with views of Mt. Baker, Bellingham Bay, and the marina at Squalicum Harbor.

SNOW SPORTS

The Mt. Baker Ski Area provides Whatcom County residents with a place to ski, snowboard, or sled. It is noted for one of the longest ski seasons in the state, often opening in November and closing in April. From Bellingham, head 52 miles east on Highway 542. It's about an hour and a quarter drive to the ski area. Direct your questions to the Mt. Baker business office, 734-6771. To find out about snow conditions, call 671-0211.

Lift Tickets

Cost of lift tickets on weekends and holidays: Adult (16 and over) $30; Youth (ages 7-15) $22.50; Child (6 and under) Free
Cost of lift tickets Monday-Wednesday (non-holiday): Adult $18.50; Youth $14; Child Free
Cost of lift tickets Thursday & Friday (non-holiday): Adult $20; Youth $15; Child Free
Beginner chair lift (#2 only): All ages $18.50
Beginner rope tow: Free
Fifth Grade Free Lift Ticket Program: Fifth graders who are enrolled in this program get free lift tickets any time they visit Mt. Baker during the ski season. What a deal! Fill out an application to enroll. Call the Mt. Baker business office for more information.

There are two main ski areas at Mt. Baker: White Salmon and Heather Meadows. White Salmon is at an elevation of 3,500 feet and features a new day lodge that has ski and snowboard rentals, retail services, lift ticket sales, and a restaurant. A rope tow and chair lifts are here. The Heather Meadows ski area is a bit higher with an elevation of 4,300 feet. It has a rope tow, chair lifts, and a 4 km loop trail for cross country skiers. Its day lodge sells lift tickets and has a restaurant and child care center. Call the Mt. Baker business office to inquire about available child care. The Mountain Shop next door rents and repairs skis and snowboards and has a retail shop. Come here if you need some tips on skiing or snowboarding. The Mountain Shop sells introductory packages for new skiers or snowboarders. These packages include a one and a half hour lesson, full day rentals, and beginner lift tickets. The introductory ski package is $36 for adults (16 and over) and $33 for youth (ages 8-15). The snowboard package is $43 for adults and $41 for youth. Daily ski or snowboard clinics are also held here.

If your family just wants to come up and go sledding, the most popular area is just past the Heather Meadows day lodge. Look for lines of cars parked on either side of the road. This isn't an official sledding area, so use caution. You need to haul your children and sleds up a short, steep snow bank before you get to the good sledding area. We took our toddler and preschooler here and didn't have any problem negotiating the snow bank. Be sure to dress warmly and bring plenty of snacks and hot beverages.

SWIMMING

W hen the weather heats up, many Whatcom County residents head to their favorite river or lake to cool off. The following outdoor swimming areas are supervised by lifeguards during the summer.

Bloedel Donovan Park
2214 Electric Ave., Bellingham; 676-6985

Cornwall Park (wading pool only)
2800 Cornwall Ave., Bellingham; 676-6985

Fairhaven Park (wading pool only)
107 Chuckanut Dr., Bellingham; 676-6985

Lake Padden Park
4882 Samish Way, Bellingham; 676-6985

Samish Park
673 N. Lake Samish Dr., Bellingham; 733-2363

Birch Bay Waterslides
4874 Birch Bay-Lynden Rd., Birch Bay; 371-7500

Hours: Open seasonally, 10:30am-7:30pm, late May through early September. Call for specific dates.
Fees: Children (6 and up) $10.95; Preschoolers (3-5 years old) $7.95; Toddlers (2 years old and under) Free with an adult

The waterslides at Birch Bay are a big thrill for kids, whether they're timid preschoolers or adventurous teens. For young children who aren't ready for the big slides, Birch Bay offers two different kiddie pools. These pools have shallow slides into shallow water. Lifeguards are on duty, but nearby signs remind parents that it's their responsibility to watch their children. Near the kiddie pools is a playground with ramps and slides.

For the thrill seekers in your family, Birch Bay offers a sixty foot drop slide which shoots people practically straight down its ramp, or "The Black Hole," which is a forty-five foot tube slide. For people who are in between the kiddie pool and terror, Birch Bay has four giant waterslides called the Snake, Corkscrew, Hairpin, and Twister. Our family went here mid-day on a sunny Saturday in summer, and while it was busy, it never seemed too crowded. The lines for the slides moved fairly quickly. Attendants were stationed at each slide to make sure the safety rules were strictly enforced.

Lounge chairs and picnic tables are scattered around the park. Many families come and spend the day. There are men's and women's changing rooms with showers, but no family changing room. A concession stand and restaurant are also located in the park.

If you just want to come in and watch your kids play, be prepared to hand over some money. Viewer rates, as they are called, are $7.50. When you enter the park you need to pay the full admission fee of $10.95. A paper bracelet is attached to your wrist. Upon your return, you give back the bracelet and you are refunded $3.45.

Books

Families in Whatcom County love to read, and we flock to bookstores and libraries. While we do have chain stores such as Barnes & Noble, Waldenbooks, and B Dalton, I wanted to focus on businesses that are unique to Whatcom County. In this chapter I included the independent bookstores in our area that carry the best selection of books for children.

Village Books
1210 11ᵗʰ St.; Bellingham; 671-2626 or 1-800-392-BOOK

Hours: Monday-Saturday 9am-10pm; Sunday 10am-8pm,
10pm in summer

Families have been coming to this large independent bookstore since 1980 for its excellent selection of new and used children's books and for its convivial atmosphere. It's the kind of place you go for the afternoon to browse through books and then have lunch at the Colophon Cafe which is inside the bookstore. Downstairs is the Bargain Book Annex where you can pick up used and remaindered books. The children's section there has picture books as well as chapter books for sale. Authors make frequent visits to Village Books, with Tomie dePaola, Jean Craighead George, and Tor Seidler examples of recent guests. Every fall—during National Children's Book Week—this store sponsors a children's book mark contest whereby the winners get their drawings reproduced as bookmarks which are then available for free at area schools and libraries.

What I like best about Village Books is that the people who work there are avid readers and can recommend books for every age and taste. If you've plowed through the *Little House on the Prairie* series and are wondering what to read next to your child, come here. You'll get some dandy ideas.

Henderson Books
112 Grand, Bellingham; 734-6855

Hours: Thursday-Saturday 9am-6pm; Sunday 11am-6pm. Closed Monday-Wednesday, plus the month of March.

Henderson's has expanded in recent years, and its huge selection of used and (some) new books is an asset to readers in Whatcom County. Books for children fill two rooms and are well organized. Popular authors such as L.M. Montgomery, Ann Martin, and R.L. Stine each have a large section devoted to them. Picture books are arranged alphabetically by author. Henderson's also carries the largest selection of Dover books in the county. Families can purchase used educational videos here, too.

Stremler Boekhandel
655 Front St., Lynden; 354-1001

Hours: Monday-Saturday 9am-5:30pm (8pm on Friday nights). Closed Sunday.

If your family is making a trip to Lynden, be sure to stop here. This small bookstore carries a good selection of books for children. There are sturdy board books for babies and appealing paperbacks for older children. Klutz books and Usborne Kid Kits are also available. These items supply readers with instructions and all the necessary supplies for learning about topics such as juggling or making door alarms that buzz.

LIBRARIES IN WHATCOM COUNTY

Most libraries offer programs for toddlers and preschoolers once a week. These programs usually include stories, activities, and songs. Many libraries also offer monthly programs for school age children that include stories and crafts. Call your local library for more information.

Bellingham Public Library
210 Central Ave.; 676-6860
Hours: Monday-Thursday 10am-9pm; Friday & Saturday 10am-6pm; Sunday (September-May) 1pm-5pm

Blaine Library
610 3rd St.; 332-8146
Hours: Monday & Tuesday 10am-6pm; Wednesday & Thursday 10am-9pm; Friday & Saturday 10am-6pm

Deming Library
5044 Mt. Baker Hwy.; 592-2422
Hours: Monday 10am-9pm; Tuesday & Thursday 10am-9pm; Saturday 10am-5pm

Everson Library
104 Kirsch Dr.; 966-5100
Hours: Monday 10am-6pm; Tuesday & Wednesday 10am-9pm; Thursday 1pm-9pm; Friday & Saturday 10am-6pm

Fairhaven Library
1117 12th St.; 676-6877
Hours: Monday-Saturday 1pm-6pm

Ferndale Library
2222 Main St.; 384-3647
Hours: Monday-Thursday 10am-9pm; Friday & Saturday 10am-6pm

Island Library (Lummi Island)
2144 S. Nugent Rd.; 758-7145
Hours: Thursday 2:30pm-8:30pm; Friday & Saturday 11am-4pm

Lynden Library
205 4th St.; 354-4883
Hours: Monday-Thursday 10am-9pm; Friday & Saturday 10am-6pm

Maple Falls Library
7509 Mt. Baker Hwy.; 599-2020
Hours: Wednesday 10am-7pm; Saturday 10am-5pm

Point Roberts Library
Community Center on Gulf Rd.; 945-6545
Hours: Tuesday 4pm-8pm; Wednesday 12pm-6pm; Saturday 10am-4pm

Sumas Library
451 2nd St.; 988-2501
Hours: Monday & Wednesday 12pm-9pm; Saturday 12pm-5pm

Public Reference Center
5205 Northwest Rd.; Bellingham; 384-3150
Hours: Monday-Saturday 10am-5pm

Arts & Crafts

If a child in your family is an artist or just likes to mess around with paper, glue, and crayons, take him or her to one of the following places.

Bead Bazaar
1001 Harris Ave., Fairhaven; 671-5655

Hours: Monday-Saturday 10am-6:30pm; Sunday 12pm-5:30pm

If you've never been in a bead store before, be prepared to spend a lot of time just *looking*. Beads come in a vast assortment of sizes, colors, and materials. If you're feeling overwhelmed and need some ideas to help you get started, the store has many samples of necklaces, earrings, and bracelets already made up. Check out the handy tip sheets near the door if you want to know how to make earrings or attach a clasp. Besides beads, this store also carries charms, medallions, and all the necessary supplies for creative jewelry making.

Dakota Art Store
1411 Cornwall Ave., Bellingham; 676-8918

Hours: Monday-Saturday 9am-6pm; Sunday 12pm-5pm

Whether your child is a serious art student or just likes to make things, Dakota Art Store is an exciting place to come. Many local artists buy their supplies here. This store stocks many of the Creativity for Kids kits. These boxed kits contain everything your child will need to make such projects as hand painted ceramic tiles, memory stones, or hand made paper. Dakota Art also carries Dover activity books, Dorling Kindersley stickers, rubber stamps, and origami paper. When my daughter and I stopped there recently, we felt compelled to buy small bags of colored miniature popsicle sticks and chenille pipe cleaners. We didn't know what we were going to make with them, but we knew we'd figure out something!

PAINT YOUR OWN CERAMIC STUDIOS

Whatcom County has two main paint your own ceramic studios. Paint Expressions is located in Fairhaven and Planet Picasso is located in Barkley Village. Each carries a wide selection of unpainted ceramic pieces, which range from traditional plates, bowls, and mugs to more whimsical items such as animal figurines or moon shaped boxes. Each studio supplies its customers with paint, brushes, stencils, and idea books. Finished pieces are ready to be picked up in a few days. Fees are structured differently at each studio.

My daughter has decorated mugs at both places. She had a grand time and her mugs came out, well...colorful!

Paint Expressions
1308 A. 11ᵗʰ St., Bellingham; 752-1724

Hours: Every day 11am-6pm
Cost: $6 and up

This studio occupies the same storefront as the Abbey Garden Tea Room. Enjoy a pot of tea or hot chocolate while you create your masterpiece. Paint Expressions carries over 200 unpainted ceramic pieces. The price listed on each piece includes paint in as many colors as you wish, firing, and glazing. Piggy banks and tiles are popular choices with children.

Planet Picasso

2950 Newmarket St., Suite 101, Bellingham; 738-1188

Hours: Tuesday-Thursday 10am-7pm; Friday & Saturday 10am-9pm; Sunday 12pm-7pm. Closed Monday.
Cost: $8 and up

This cheerful studio offers specials during the week. On Tuesdays you get two of the same ceramic piece for the price of one. On Thursdays kids paint free. At Planet Picasso customers choose their ceramic piece which may range in price from $2 to $42, then are charged studio time. The fee is $6/person for the first hour and then pro-rated after that. The studio fee includes the unlimited use of five paint colors, glazing, and firing. Animal figurines are popular with kids.

Paper Zone

915 Iowa St., Bellingham; 671-3755

Hours: Monday-Friday 8am-6pm; Saturday 8am-5pm; Sunday 11am-4pm

It's hard to imagine all the forms paper can take until you come to a place such as this. The Paper Zone carries products made out of, you guessed it, paper! The store is organized into sections: Fine Papers, Art, Cards, Party, and Office. Whether you are looking for paper items for a party, handmade paper for that special art project, or zany stationery to send to a best friend, you can find it here. Paper Zone now carries rubber stamps and inks, too.

Stampadoodle
915 Iowa St., Bellingham; 647-9663

Hours: Monday-Thursday 10am-6pm; Friday & Saturday 10am-7pm; Sunday 11am-5pm

This store carries every kind of rubber stamp you can imagine and, if they don't, they can custom make one. Children's passions are well represented here. Stampadoodle carries a large selection of horse and animal stamps, sport stamps, Disney stamps, and music stamps. If your family would like to design its own Christmas or birthday cards, this is the place to come. I counted fifty different Christmas stamps in one section. Besides stamps, this store also carries stickers, stencils, and fabric ink. If you want a special paper to use for your project, check out the Paper Zone next door.

Birthday fun at Stampadoodle. Photo courtesy of Stampadoodle.

95

Student Co-op Bookstore
Western Washington University; 650-3655

Hours: Monday-Friday 7:30am-5pm; Saturday 11am-3pm. Closed Sunday.

If your child loves to poke around art stores, take a trip to the bookstore on Western's campus. The art supply section is located on the second floor and has all sorts of goodies to spark your child's imagination. The last time I was there, I spotted a mini-pad of construction paper, a kit to make a plaster of Paris mold of your hand, and hand-made paper with flowers embedded in it. The prices on art supplies are very reasonable here. They also carry a wide variety of markers, pens, colored pencils, and pastels.

The most convenient place to park is in the metered lot below the Viking Union. The meters are good for two hours and cost a dollar an hour. To reach the lot, turn off Garden Street onto Pine.

Ferries, Boats, Buses & Trains

K ids love to ride on different forms of transportation, and Whatcom County provides them with many opportunities. Spend the day on a boat cruising the waters around the San Juan Islands looking for whales, hop on board the Whatcom Chief and ride over to Lummi Island for the day, make a loop into Fairhaven and back on one of the new trolley buses, or ride on a passenger train that was built in the 1920s.

Lummi Island Ferry
Gooseberry Point; 676-6759

Schedule: Ferries leave from Gooseberry Point at ten minutes past the hour and leave from Lummi Island on the hour. More runs are added during peak commute times.
Fares: $2/regular sized vehicle; $1/person. Fares are only collected on the trip to Lummi Island. The return trip is free.
Driving Directions: From I-5 take the Slater Road Exit (260). Drive west on Slater Road 3.7 miles to Haxton Way and turn left. Follow Haxton Way 6.7 miles to the ferry terminal at Gooseberry Point.

Many people who live in Whatcom County on the mainland have never been to Lummi Island, an eight minute ferry crossing from Gooseberry Point. It's worth the trip, especially on a clear day. The view of the San Juan Islands from the west side of Lummi is spectacular. Orcas Island lies straight across the water, three nautical miles away.

Although Lummi Indians were the island's first inhabitants, many had left before the first white settlers arrived in the 1870s. The Lummis fled to avoid the fierce northern Indian tribes who used to paddle south to raid other tribes. Today Lummi Island, which is not part of the Lummi Reservation but is part of the San Juans, has over 600 residents, many of whom are artists. These artists open their studios three times a year to the public. Tours are held the weekends before Memorial Day and Labor Day, and on the first weekend in December.

A good way to see Lummi Island is by bicycle. From the ferry dock turn right on Nugent Road. Continue on this road. It will turn into West Shore Drive near the northern tip of the island. Continue on West Shore Drive. It will eventually turn into Legoe Bay Road. Continue on Legoe Bay Road until you come to Nugent Road again. Turn left. The ferry dock is a short way down this road. This loop ride will take you by the community center of Lummi, which is spread out around the ferry dock, and past Beach School, Lummi Island's only public school. The views of the San Juan Islands from West Shore Drive and Legoe Bay are outstanding. Of course, you can also drive this loop in your car; the timing is just right for those on a tight schedule. You have time to get off the ferry, drive the loop, and stop by the Islander Store for a popsicle before catching the next boat. If you have more time to spend on Lummi Island, you might want to stop at the following places.

Beach School
3786 Centerview Rd.; 383-9440

This school is part of the Ferndale School District and provides services to the island's elementary school students. Older students catch the ferry to attend school in Ferndale. Beach School's playground has basketball hoops, swings, a climbing structure, and a slide. Visitors may use the playground after school hours or on weekends.

Beach Store Cafe
2200 N. Nugent Rd.; 758-2233

Summer Hours (Memorial Day-Labor Day): Open six days a week, 9am-9pm. Closed Tuesday. Call for winter hours.

This cafe has a spectacular view of Mt. Baker looming across Hale's Passage. It also has a menu that should

99

appeal to all members of your family. See page 125 for a more thorough description of this friendly restaurant.

Islander Store
2106 S. Nugent Rd.; 758-2190

Hours: Sunday-Thursday 6:30am-10:30pm; Friday & Saturday 6:30am-11:30pm. Closes one hour earlier in winter.

This store sells groceries, coffee, and snacks. The Lummi Island Farmer's Market is held outside on Saturday mornings during the summer.

Island Library
2144 S. Nugent Rd.; 758-7145
Hours: Thursday 2:30pm-8:30pm; Friday & Saturday 11am-4pm

Lummi Island Overlook
This large wooden platform with benches is located right across the street from The Beach Store Cafe. Visitors have marvelous views of water, Mt. Baker, and the Canadian Coast Range. Stairs lead down to one of the only public beaches on Lummi Island.

PASSENGER FERRIES TO THE SAN JUAN ISLANDS

San Juan Island Shuttle Express

Bellingham Cruise Terminal; 355 Harris Ave., Bellingham
671-1137 or 1-888-373-8522

Summer Schedule: Leave Bellingham at **9:15am** daily. Arrive Friday Harbor, San Juan Island **11:30am.** Depart Friday Harbor at **4:00pm.** Arrive Bellingham **6:15pm.**
Cost (round trip): Adult $33; Senior $29; Children (17 and under) $27
Cost for Whale Watch: Adult $60; Children (17 and under) $45

The Shuttle Express provides passenger service to the San Juan Islands.

101

San Juan Island Commuter

Bellingham Cruise Terminal; 734-8180 or 1-888-734-8180

Summer Schedule: Leave Bellingham at **10am** daily. Arrive Friday Harbor at **12pm**. Depart Friday Harbor at **4:30pm**. Arrive Bellingham at **6:30pm**.
Cost (round trip): Adult $35; Children (ages 6-12) $17.50; Children (ages 5 and under) Free

During the summer two passenger-only ferries, The San Juan Island Commuter and the San Juan Island Shuttle Express, carry people from Bellingham to the San Juans. This is a convenient way to get to the islands if you have somebody to pick you up at your destination. It also makes a wonderful day trip to explore the town of Friday Harbor on San Juan Island. Both boats sell snacks and beverages on board and provide restrooms.

The ferries leave from the Bellingham Cruise Terminal once a day and take approximately the same length of time to reach Friday Harbor—two hours. Once there, passengers may disembark and spend the afternoon exploring Friday Harbor before returning to Bellingham in late afternoon. If you ride the Shuttle Express, you have the option of getting off in Friday Harbor or remaining on board to go whale watching. If you choose the latter activity, it will cost an extra $27 for adults and $18 for children.

My daughter and I rode on the Shuttle Express and the Island Commuter during the summer of 1998. Of the two, the Shuttle Express was the more comfortable and kid friendly. During the ride we sat at a booth with a table, colored, played Go Fish, and looked out the window. A crew member offered my daughter crayons and a picture to color. On the Island Commuter we sat side by side with the other passengers in a U formation around the boat. The seating was quite high and neither of us could reach the ground with our feet. We had a small table nearby on which we could color or play cards.

Both boats let us off at the marina in Friday Harbor. From there, it's a quick walk into town. Our four hour shore leave went quickly. We enjoyed the following places and activities.

The Whale Museum
62 First St.; 378-4710 or 1-800-946-7227

Cost: Adults $5; Seniors $4; Kids $2; Children (under 5) Free

This museum, the first in the country dedicated solely to whales, is a must see. Visitors can learn about these giant mammals by looking at exhibits, artifacts, models, and skeletons. Much of the museum's focus is on the resident pods of Orca whales that live in the waters around the San Juan Islands.

Osito's
310 Spring St.; 378-4320

I wish Osito's was in Bellingham! This charming store carries high quality children's toys, books, and clothing. We spent nearly an hour here just looking around. For the trip home, we decided to buy a pad of paper and markers that change colors.

The Toy Box
Cannery Landing; 378-8889
This store carries a good selection of puzzles, games, and activity books.

Griffin Bay Bookstore
40 First St.; 378-5511
The children's section is physically small, but packed with as many books as possible.

Harbor Bookstore
24 Cannery Landing; 378-7222
Harbor Bookstore is well stocked with nature books for children.

Madelyn's Bagel Bakery
225 A St.; 378-4545
Madelyn's offers at least a dozen different kinds of bagels to go with your coffee, tea, or juice.

Katrina's
135 2nd St.; 378-7290
Katrina's is known for its homemade soups, salads, breads, and desserts. Try the spinach pie, a house speciality. Kids can order hot dogs, nachos, or bread, cheese, and fruit.

The Doctor's Office
85 Front St.; 378-8865
This Doctor's Office is located in a green house across the street from the Washington State Ferry dock and sells homemade ice cream. Sit on the front steps and watch all the hubbub in Friday Harbor.

WHALE WATCH CRUISES

While the *Island Caper* is the most popular boat for whale watching, families can also choose to ride on the San Juan Island Shuttle Express. The *Island Caper* departs Squalicum Harbor at 10am and spends the day cruising prime whale watching waters. The Shuttle Express takes passengers to Friday Harbor where they can choose to get off for a shore leave or remain on board to go whale watching. For more information about the San Juan Island Shuttle Express turn to page 102.

San Juan Island Shuttle Express
Bellingham Cruise Terminal; 671-1137 or 1-888-373-8522

Schedule: Leave Bellingham at **9:15am** daily. Arrive Friday Harbor at **11:30am**. Depart Friday Harbor for whale watch at **12:30pm**. Arrive back to Friday Harbor at **3:30pm**. Leave Friday Harbor for Bellingham at **4:30pm** and arrive back at **6:15pm**.
Cost for whale watch: Adult $60; Children (17 and under) $45

Island Mariner Cruises
#5 Harbor Esplanade, Bellingham; 734-8866

Schedule: Depart Bellingham at **10am** and return at **5pm** every Saturday and Sunday from late May through early September, plus every Tuesday and Thursday in July and August.
Cost: Adults $55; Seniors (62 and up) $45; Children (15 and under) $35

The *Island Caper* is a large, comfortable boat on which to spend the day searching for whales in the San Juan Islands. Families can sit inside at the many tables or lounge on couches or in easy chairs. Bench seating is available on the top deck. If you choose to sit up there, be sure to bring warm jackets and hats, even if the day is sunny and warm. It gets colder than you think out on the water. The *Island Caper* sees Orca whales on nearly ninety percent of its trips. Unfortunately, on the day we went we didn't see any of them. However, we did see seals, eagles, Dahl's porpoises, and a Minke whale. Even though we didn't see any Orcas, we did enjoy ourselves. The scenery through the San Juans is spectacular. I took my four year old and we brought along books, tapes, and playing cards to help pass the time.

Families can bring their own food aboard or purchase items from the concession area. We brought a large picnic lunch and then splurged on M&Ms and juice. Besides candy and beverages, customers can purchase bagels and cream cheese, hot dogs, garden burgers, or mini-pizzas.

Even though we didn't see Orcas, I am planning to go again. The scenery alone is worth the trip; seeing Orcas would be a bonus.

Plover

Blaine Visitor's Dock, Blaine; 332-4544

Dates: End of May-early September
Hours: Friday & Saturday 12pm-9pm; Sunday 10am-6pm.
Departs on the hour from the Blaine Visitor's Dock. Departs on
the half hour from the wharf at the Inn at Semiahmoo.
Cost: Free, but donations cheerfully accepted
Driving Directions: From I-5 take the Blaine City Center exit
(276). Head west under the freeway, turn right on Marine Drive,
and follow the signs.

This was one of my favorite finds last summer. We don't
get out on boats much, so it was a real treat to be out
on the water. And you can't beat the cost—free! The *Plover* is a restored foot passenger ferry that used to take
cannery workers from Blaine to the now defunct Alaska
Packers Association Salmon Cannery on Semiahmoo Spit.
It is certified to hold seventeen passengers. Bicycles and

The Plover

107

strollers are accommodated on a space available basis. Passengers can stand on the top deck or sit below and look out the window. Either way, visitors are treated to some wonderful sights. The westbound trip to Semiahmoo takes a little over ten minutes and the return trip about twenty. En route, passengers see Blaine Harbor, Mt. Baker, the Canadian Coast Range, resident harbor seals, plenty of seagulls, and other local water birds such as cormorants and Caspian Terns. I took my four year old and she loved it—especially the baby gulls and seals. I was glad my active eighteen month old was home with Dad. The boat is small and there's not a lot of room to chase a busy toddler.

BUSES

B uses in Whatcom County are inexpensive, can take you almost anywhere, and are a thrill for young children to ride.

Whatcom Transportation Authority

Bellingham Transit Center; Magnolia & Railroad Ave.
676-RIDE or 354-RIDE

Cost: People (ages 8-65) 50 cents; Seniors (age 65 and up) 25 cents; Children (age 7 and under) Free

F or a short, scenic trip, try bus Number 1, which takes you from the Bellingham Transit Center to Fairhaven and back in just half an hour. This route travels along State Street and kids can look out the window and watch all the action on Bellingham Bay. This is a good route anyway, but what makes it even better is the fact that one of the handsome, new trolley buses makes this trip. Buses run every thirty minutes on this route, so sometimes we like to ride the trolley into Fairhaven, have a snack, and then ride back. For kid-friendly activities in Fairhaven, see page 149.

TRAINS

All right, all right, a fascination with trains probably *is* biological. Our son loves them and his sister couldn't care less. For the train aficionados in your family, here's a list of favorite places to see or ride on trains.

Amtrak Train

Fairhaven Station; 401 Harris, Bellingham
1-800-872-7245 or 734-8851

The Amtrak departs Bellingham northbound at 9:52am and southbound at 7:27pm. While you're at the Fairhaven Station have a cup of hot chocolate or coffee at **Fairhaven Station Coffee and News,** 676-7166, or look at the murals on the walls inside the terminal.

Roeder Avenue

Sometimes we just drive down Roeder Avenue in Bellingham to see the box cars, lumber cars, tank cars, engines, and cabooses which are always parked along the tracks. If we're lucky, we see engines hooking up to other cars.

The Peace Train

Peach Arch Factory Outlets
Exit 270 off I-5, Custer; 366-3128

Hours: Saturday & Sunday 11am-4:30pm

Cost: $1/day pass or free ride with a $10 purchase at any of the outlet stores.

This miniature train runs on tracks around the outlet mall. It doesn't run during inclement weather, so plan on riding it some nice, sunny day.

Lake Whatcom Railway
PO Box 91, Acme; 595-2218

Hours: The train usually runs three times a day (11am, 1pm, & 3pm) on Tuesdays and Saturdays during the summer. It usually makes special trips for Valentine's Day, Easter, and Christmas, too. Call to make reservations and to confirm dates and times. **Cost:** Adults $10; Children (under 18) $5

Frank Culp has been operating his Lake Whatcom Railway since 1972. This old-time passenger train takes its customers along the 3.5 miles of right-of-way track that Mr. Culp purchased from Burlinghton Northern. The trip takes about an hour and a half, but the train isn't moving the whole time. It chugs its way past Mirror Lake and stops for twenty minutes at a small park where passengers may get off and walk around or get up in the cab of the engine. Since there isn't any place for the train to turn around to get back to the station, it has to stop while the engine is unhooked from the front of the train and brought around to be hooked up to the back of the train. It's fun to watch as the engine travels by on a parallel track. During the trip, passengers may look out the window, walk from car to car, or enjoy a small bite in the coffee car where beverages and snacks are for sale.

Western Washington University

The west was being settled in the late 1800s and Washington needed certified teachers. In 1893 the Legislature authorized the creation of a normal school in Bellingham, and in the fall of 1899 the first classes were held in Old Main. The New Whatcom Normal School, as it was called when it first opened, graduated its first class in the spring of 1900. Over the next 100 years the school expanded and changed its name several times. Western Washington University is now a regional university that offers degrees from six different colleges. Many of the state's teachers still receive their training on this beautiful campus.

Western Washington University

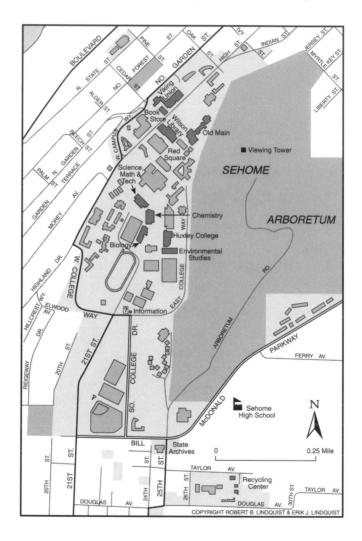

WESTERN WASHINGTON UNIVERSITY

Western is a great place to come with kids; its handsome campus is full of things to do and see. Visit the Environmental Studies Building and see dinosaur eggs and bones; take a tour of one of the nation's largest outdoor sculpture collections; check out the art supplies in the Student Co-op Bookstore; hike through Sehome Arboretum; or enjoy a dish of frozen yogurt. On evenings and weekends in the summer, the campus is especially quiet and its many paved walkways and plazas make it a pleasant place to ride bikes without worrying about cars. For more information about Western, call 650-3000. The campus operator can direct your call to the right office.

Old Main was the first building on WWU's campus.

113

Parking

If you are coming to Western Monday through Friday between 7am and 5pm, your best bet to find parking is to stop at the Visitor's Center (650-3424) on the south end of campus. The Center has a drive-up window so you don't have to get out of your car. The person on duty will direct you to the parking lot closest to your destination and give you a permit to hang from your rear view mirror. Fees are $1 an hour or $6 to park all day.

Metered parking is available in the lot below the Viking Union. I usually park here if I'm going to the library or the bookstore. The meters are good for two hours and cost a dollar an hour. To reach this lot, turn off Garden Street on to Pine Street.

Parking is free on the streets around the college, but it's often a hassle trying to find an open space. Be sure to read the signs near your car if you do find a parking space, since some areas near Western are restricted to residential parking and a special sticker is required to park there.

Buses are also a handy way to reach the university. They run frequently and you don't have to worry about finding a parking space. Call 676-RIDE or 354-RIDE for more information.

Parking is free in Western's lots on the weekends and after 5pm on weekdays. Some lots do have restrictions on them, so be sure to read the signs posted in the lots to make sure its O.K. to park there. The C lots around the Visitor's Center are usually a safe bet.

NOTABLE BUILDINGS AND FEATURES

The following is a list of buildings and features on Western's campus that will appeal to families.

Viking Union

Hours: Monday-Friday 7am-11pm; Saturday 9am-12pm; Sunday 10am-11pm

At the information booth located inside the front doors, you will find, much to the delight of most children, bins of inexpensive candy. Hershey kisses are a nickel, Bazooka Bubble Gum, both sugared and sugarless, is a dime. Pieces of black or red licorice are a nickel. We often stop here on our tour of campus. This building also has bathrooms, a cash machine, and places to eat inside on rainy days.

Student Co-op Bookstore
650-3655

Hours: Monday-Friday 7:30am-5pm; Saturday 11am-3pm. Closed Sunday.

When you walk into this store you realize that much of what appeals to college kids also appeals to children. Racks of stuffed animals, key chains, cards, and candy are on display near the cash registers. Be sure to check out the kid's book section also located on the first floor. Western trains many teachers and its bookstore carries an interesting variety of children's books. If your child's idea of heaven is to poke around art and office supply stores, head upstairs. Prices are very reasonable and they have some neat art supplies. On a recent trip I saw mini-pads of construction paper, a kit to make a plaster of Paris mold

115

of your hand, and handmade paper with flowers embedded in it. The store also carries a wide variety of markers, pens, colored pencils, and pastels.

Wilson Library
650-3050
Hours: Monday-Thursday 7:45am-11pm; Friday 7:45am-5pm; Saturday 10am-6pm; Sunday 1pm-11pm

The University's library isn't filled only with adult tomes and reference books. Due to Western's large education department, Wilson Library has a well stocked children's book section. Community members can pay a yearly fee of $25 to check out books here.

The Fountain
Located in Red Square, this large circular fountain is always a draw for kids.

Science, Mathematics, and Technology Education Building
Hours: Monday/Wednesday/Thursday 8:30am-5:30pm; Tuesday 8:30am-4:30pm; Friday 8:30am-3pm. Closed weekends.

The display case on the south side of the first floor holds some interesting items. Inside are a stuffed puffin, mountain lion, and muskrat. You can also see a few animal skeletons and a butterfly collection. Upstairs from this display is the Learning Resource Center, Room 220. This spacious, cheerful room is often filled with college students working on projects, but it's O.K. to take your kids in as long as they're quiet. Up here you can see a stuffed

Bald Eagle, Trumpeter Swan, and owl. Sea creatures such as a dried blowfish, a turtle, and a preserved octopus are also on display as are whale vertebrae and small animal skeletons.

Glass Bridge

You can walk between the Chemistry and Biology Buildings on a glassed in bridge located on the fourth floor. It's fun to be able to go from one building to the next without walking on the ground.

Environmental Studies Building

Hours: Monday-Friday 7am-9:30pm; Saturday 7:30am-6pm; Sunday & Holidays 7:30am-11pm

This building holds a trove of treasures. On the first floor, rocks and minerals are on display along with information about the mining history in Whatcom County. Head to the second floor to see fossilized dinosaur eggs, a twenty thousand year old Columbian Mammoth tusk, or a cast taken from footprints of a rhinoceros-like mammal that lived fifty million years ago. The tusk and the tracks were both found within fifty miles of Bellingham! These are just a few of the gems this building holds. Plan on an expedition trip here soon.

Sehome Hill Arboretum
25th St. & Bill McDonald Parkway, Bellingham; 676-6985

Highlights: Hiking, native plants, viewing tower

Sehome Hill is a 165 acre native plant arboretum jointly owned by Western Washington University and the City of Bellingham. Visitors can hike on its trails and see Douglas fir, alder, big leaf maple, Oregon grape, Indian plum, snowberry, and salal.

For a marvelous view of the city of Bellingham, the San Juans, and the Canadian Coastal Range, head for the viewing tower at the top of the hill. Families can reach it by hiking the whole way (approximately one mile) or by driving most of the way and walking a short distance. To begin the hike, park at the trailhead located off Bill McDonald Parkway. The main trail is well marked. Follow the signs to the tower. If you'd rather drive, steer your car past the trailhead parking lot and head up Arboretum Drive. Park in the lot on top and follow the signs to the tower. It's about a five minute walk.

SCULPTURES
Western is home to an acclaimed outdoor sculpture collection. To learn more about these sculptures, stop by the Visitor's Center to pick up a brochure or to inquire about the free audiophone tour. The Visitor's Center is open Monday-Friday 7am-5pm. Here are some of the sculptures that appeal especially to children.

The Man Who Used to Hunt Cougars for Bounty

This granite sculpture by Richard Beyer is located out side of Wilson Library and depicts a man and a cougar. It is a favorite with many visitors.

For Handel

Mark di Suvero's orange painted steel sculpture rises gracefully outside the plaza at the Performing Arts Center.

Skyviewing Sculpture

This tilted iron cube with cutout circles is the sculpture that Western pictures on many of its brochures. It's located in Red Square by Miller Hall and was created by Isamu Noguchi.

Wright's Triangle

Richard Serra's open steel triangles near the Ross Engineering Technology Building allow visitors to walk in and out of the sculpture.

Log Ramps

Lloyd Hamrol's log ramps are made out of Douglas fir and Western Red Cedar. When kids see this sculpture, located near the Chemisty Building, they naturally want to run up it. Let them.

Stone Enclosure: Rock Rings

This beautiful sculpture created by Nancy Holt is made out of brown mountain stone and looks like something you'd find in the fields of England. Kids love to walk through the arches and climb into the circular openings. It's located in a big, grassy field behind the Environmental Studies Building.

Untitled (Steam Work for Bellingham)

When people see steam rising from the grass near the walkway to Fairhaven College, they usually stop and investigate. The steam is an ethereal sculpture by Robert Morris who used the steam conduit system to Fairhaven College to help him produce his art. Sometimes you see this sculpture, sometimes you don't.

Stone Enclosure by Nancy Holt

FOOD

College students like to eat, so there are plenty of places to buy inexpensive food on campus. However, most of the eateries are only open Monday through Friday. Only Plaza Pizza and "TCBY" Yogurt are open on Saturday and Sunday.

Plaza Pizza
Viking Addition Plaza Level
Hours: Monday-Friday 11am-10pm; Saturday and Sunday 11am-9pm

Here you can buy pizza by the slice, ready made sal ads, pastries, and beverages. After 5pm a potato bar is also offered.

"TCBY" Yogurt at Bigfoot's Bistro
Viking Addition 3rd floor
Hours: Monday-Friday 11am-10pm; Saturday and Sunday 2pm-10pm

Enjoy a wonderful view of Bellingham Bay while you eat your frozen yogurt.

Creative Juices
Viking Addition Plaza Level
Hours: Monday-Friday 7:30am-3pm. Closed weekends.

Freshly squeezed fruit and vegetable drinks are served here along with healthy snacks.

Cyberwraps
Viking Addition Plaza Level inside Creative Juices
Hours: Monday-Friday 10:30am-2:30pm. Closed weekends.

Wraps are huge and inexpensive. Try the Greek or Thai Wrap or stick with the Basic Wrap—brown rice, beans, cheese.

Miller's Coffee House
Miller Hall First Floor
Hours: Monday-Friday 7:30am-7:30pm. Closed weekends.

Miller's offers ready-made salads, sandwiches, soups, bagels, and beverages.

Arntzen's Atrium & Espresso
Arntzen Hall First Floor
Hours: Monday-Thursday 7:30am-7:30pm; Friday 7:30am-3pm. Closed weekends.

Arntzen's Atrium offers the same kinds of foods as Miller's except that a Pizza Hut Express is located within the restaurant. Pizza Hut serves personal pan pizzas Monday through Friday from 10am-2pm.

Restaurants & Sweets

The places listed in this chapter emphasize food that is homemade, are friendly towards kids, and have menus that appeal to adults *and* children.

Abbey Garden Tea Room
1308 11th St., Bellingham; 752-1752

Hours: Every day 11am-6pm

The Abbey Garden Tea Room is a charming place to take your daughter, your mother, or any other special woman in your life. Yes, men come here, too, and enjoy themselves, but the Tea Room's doilies, cozies, and china tea cups seem to call to the feminine half of life. Try the Cream Tea ($4.95) which comes with a pot of tea, a scone with whipped cream and raspberry jam, and fresh fruit. Kids enjoy the Lil' Tea ($4.95) which is served with a pot of tea or cocoa, three honey butter tea sandwiches, and two tea cookies. If you'd like more substantial food, the Abbey Garden Tea Room also serves delicious soups, salads, quiches, and pasties. The Tea Room shares a space with Paint Expressions, a paint your own ceramic studio. Many people like to come here to paint while they sip tea.

The Bagelry
1319 Railroad, Bellingham; 676-5288

Hours: Monday-Friday 6:30am-5pm; Saturday 7:30am-4pm; Sunday 8am-3pm

The Bagelry makes Whatcom County's best bagels and is a popular spot with families. The prices are reasonable and the service is fast. Customers can eat their bagels plain, buttered, or smeared with cream cheese. This cafe also serves omelets, homemade soups, and deli sandwiches—made on their bagels, of course! Muffins, desserts, and beverages are also available.

Beach Store Cafe
2200 N. Nugent Rd., Lummi Island; 758-CAFE

Summer Hours (Memorial Day to Labor Day): Open six days a week 9am-9pm. Closed Tuesday. Call for winter hours.

Some sunny day, walk on board the *Whatcom Chief* ferry, take the eight minute ride to Lummi Island, and stroll over to the Beach Store Cafe. You'll be glad you did. The emphasis here is on fresh food made from local ingredients, if possible. Try their pasta dishes, homemade pizza, or fish and chips. A kid's menu is available with items such as mouse pancakes, grilled cheese sandwiches, or burgers (chicken, beef, or veggie). The cafe has large picture windows that look out over the water. Across the street, stairs lead down to the beach—one of the only public beaches on Lummi Island. To encourage you to leave your car on the mainland, the owners will reimburse you for your walk-on ferry tab. What a deal. A free ferry ride, terrific food, and a nearby beach.

125

Casa Que Pasa
1415 Railroad Ave., Bellingham; 738-TACO

Hours: Monday-Thursday 11am-11pm; Friday 11am-12pm; Sunday 11am-9pm

If your children are entering the ravenous years where they can consume a mixing bowl of cold cereal one hour after eating dinner, then this is the place to come. Really, the large portions are just an aside. Casa Que Pasa serves some of the best Mexican food in Whatcom County. The focus is on fresh foods made from scratch. Their burritoes are justifiably popular. The Vegetarian Special weighs at least one pound and comes with beans, Spanish rice, lettuce, and salsa. Meat eaters might want to try the Carne Asada burrito which is packed with grilled, marinated steak, fresh guacamole, and salsa. Lighter eaters can choose among quesadillas, tacos, or Casa Que Pasa's wonderful soups.

The Colophon Cafe
1208 11th, Bellingham; 647-0092

Hours: Monday-Saturday 9am-10pm; Sunday 10am-8pm, 10pm in the summer

The Colophon shares a space with Village Books and is noted for its terrific soups, salads, and desserts. The kid-friendly menu offers such items as peanutbutter and jelly sandwiches (with or without chocolate chips) or plain, toasted bagels. Parents might like to try the spicy African Peanut Soup or the pot pie of the day. The Colophon bakes its own desserts and serves them in oversized portions. The chocolate chunk cake could easily be split two ways and probably should be—it's huge! Customers can choose to eat upstairs, downstairs, or on nice days, outside. Upstairs has the fastest service if you're looking for a quick meal or a tasty ice cream cone.

Old Town Cafe
316 W. Holly St., Bellingham; 671-4431

Hours: Monday- Saturday 6:30am-3pm; Sunday 8am-2pm

The Old Town has been a Bellingham institution since the sixties. While it's not quite as funky as it used to be, it still retains much of its counterculture atmosphere. Carnivores, vegetarians, and vegans can all find something to eat on the menu. Portions are generous and prices are reasonable. Kids can order from their own section and get items such as half a grilled cheese sandwich or a teddy bear pancake. Old Town has a play section filled with toys and games to keep children occupied until their orders arrive.

Pepper Sisters
1055 N. State St., Bellingham; 671-3414

Hours: Tuesday- Sunday 4:30pm-9pm. Closed Monday.

Pepper Sisters is my kind of restaurant! A real adult restaurant that doesn't mind if you bring your kids along. The menu features Southwest fare prepared with fresh ingredients. Nightly specials include one seafood and one vegetarian entrée. A children's section is on the menu and beverages can be served in a sippy cup. Our family likes to go early when it's not too crowded. The waiting area in the back is a handy place to walk around with an active toddler before your meal arrives. Pepper Sisters also has a basket of toys to keep kids entertained. If your children are old enough to sit through dessert without wiggling too much, you might want to stick around and enjoy an after dinner treat. Desserts are all homemade and change frequently. You might find frozen lime cheesecake, nectarine cobbler, or golden layer cake with fudge frosting.

Stanello's Restaurant
1514 12th St., Bellingham; 676-1304

Hours: Dining room is open Monday-Thursday 4pm-10pm; Friday & Saturday 4pm-11pm; Sunday 1pm-10pm

Stanello's is a popular Fairhaven restaurant for pizza and other Italian food. Families can order a pizza from the list on the menu or create one of their own. While there isn't a specific menu available for children, kids can order small portions of pasta dishes. Stanello's also offers a carry-out service for busy families.

Swan Cafe
1220 N. Forest St., Bellingham; 734-0542

Hours: Every day 8am-8pm

This self-service cafe is located in a bright, sunny corner of the Community Food Co-op. From the deli case, customers can choose from an array of ready-made salads, sandwiches, and wraps. Soups are also available. If you just need a snack, the Swan Cafe sells a wide assortment of cookies, bars, and muffins. Customers may also purchase food items from the co-op to eat in the cafe.

My children like to come here just to look out the windows. Holly and Forest is a busy intersection in Bellingham, and a constant parade of cars, buses, and trucks roll by.

SWEETS

From homemade ice cream to chocolates to cookies, here are some tasty places to satisfy a sweet tooth.

Avenue Bread

1313 Railroad Ave., Bellingham; 676-9274

Hours: Monday-Friday 7:30am-5:30pm; Saturday 7:30am-4pm; Closed Sunday

While this friendly bakery specializes in homemade breads baked in a stone-hearth oven, they also carry a tempting array of pastries and cookies. Our family likes to buy breadsticks or cinnamon twists and then sit near the sunny picture window and watch the pigeons outside.

Bay City Ice Cream

1135 Railroad Ave., Bellingham; 676-5156

Hours: Monday- Saturday 10am-10pm; Sunday 12 pm-10pm

This ice cream parlor, located in a sunny storefront near the Bellingham Farmer's Market, features homemade ice cream. Flavors such as Bubblegum or Snickers are popular with kids. Adult flavors include Espresso Chip, Bailey's Irish Cream, and Mandarin Orange. Besides ice cream, this store carries other goodies to satisfy a sweet tooth. Customers can purchase doughnuts, cotton candy, or a small assortment of bulk candy. Deli sandwiches, hamburgers, soups, salads, and beverages are also available.

The C Shop
4825 Alderson Rd., Birch Bay; 371-2070

Hours: Open seasonally. The Candy Shop is open daily mid-June through Labor Day from 1pm-10pm. The Cafe is open during the summer Thursday-Monday from 11am (1pm on Sundays)-8pm.

If anyone in your family has a sweet tooth and you don't mind indulging it once in a while, the C Shop is a special place to come. This family owned business has been cheerfully serving its customers for over twenty-five years. The C Shop makes its own candy and chocolates. Peanut Butter Yummms and Mint Sundae are just two of their specialty items. They also carry cotton candy, caramel apples, ice cream, and snow cones made with their own syrup.

The Cafe next door features sandwiches made on their homemade bread, soups, and (after 5pm) pizzas with homemade crust and sauce. The Cafe also serves large cinnamon rolls and sticky buns, cookies, and muffins. Bake days are Monday, Thursday, and Saturday. If you've never been to the C Shop, plan a day to explore Birch Bay and then stop here.

Cookie Cafe
1319 Cornwall Ave., Bellingham; 671-8550

Hours: Monday-Friday 6am-late; Sunday 7am-late. Closing hours vary with the evening entertainment schedule.

This is a cheerful place to stop in if you're downtown and need a snack. Even though the Cookie Cafe has expanded its menu over the years to include more lunch items, their baked goods still remain popular. The Cafe offers nine different kinds of cookies, along with cream cheese brownies, cinnamon rolls, scones, and muffins. For lunch you might enjoy their soups, salads, sandwiches, or lasagna.

Ferndale Bakery
5686 3rd St., Ferndale; 384-1554

Hours: Monday-Saturday 6am-5:30pm. Closed Sunday.

The Ferndale Bakery celebrated its 25th anniversary in 1998. You don't find too many small town bakeries anymore, so the Ferndale Bakery is special in this regard. Customers can choose among doughnuts, muffins, cookies, or breads, but German pastries are their specialty. Seating is limited so if it's a nice day, you might want to take your goodies and go to Pioneer Park.

131

Lynden Dutch Bakery
421 W. Front St., Lynden; 354-3911

Hours: Monday-Saturday 5am-6pm. Closed Sunday.

The Lynden Dutch Bakery is a cheerful place—full of bustle, camaraderie, and good food. Everybody seems to know everybody else. As its name implies, this bakery specializes in Dutch fare. Krenten Bollen (raisin buns) are a top seller. Pies such as Dutch apple or Bumbleberry are also popular. Kids enjoy any of their cookies, especially the huge, aptly named, Monster Cookies. If you're not in the mood for anything sweet, you might want to order a submarine sandwich or a bowl of soup. Highchairs and a basket of toys are provided for children.

Mallard Ice Cream
207 E. Holly St., Bellingham; 734-3884

Hours: Monday-Saturday 10am-10pm; Sunday 11am-9pm

If you're a fan of high quality ice cream, whether it's in the form of a cone, shake, or sundae, come to Mallard Ice Cream. You won't be disappointed. The first time I tried their peppermint ice cream, I knew something was going to be different. Instead of the usual bright pink or green, it was white. Instead of tasting like a candy cane, it had the clean, refreshing taste of real mint. Mmmm. Mallard uses only natural ingredients in their ice cream. They make it right in the store, and if you'd like to see how it's done, tours (and tastes!) are available. Call the store to find out tour times and dates.

Seasonal Activities

No matter what season of the year, Whatcom County has special activities that families will enjoy. Kick off spring with a trip to the Bellingham Farmer's Market. In the summer attend a free concert on the lawn of the Bellingham Public Library. During the fall sample apples and grapes at Cloud Mountain Farm. Celebrate winter by making beeswax candles at the Waldorf School's Holiday Faire.

SPRING

Kick off spring by taking a trip to the Bellingham Farmer's Market. It opens the first Saturday in April. Local vendors sell flowers, produce, food, and crafts. Below is a list of all the farmer's markets in Whatcom County.

Bellingham Farmer's Market

Railroad Ave. and Chestnut St.

Dates/Hours: Every Saturday, 10am-3pm, from early April to late October. Open Sundays, 11am-3pm, June through September.

The atmosphere at the Bellingham Farmer's Market is festive, with families walking around sampling food, eating ice cream, listening to live music, talking to neighbors, and shopping for fresh produce. The last Saturday of every month is Kid's Day at the market. Kids can rent booths for $5/day to sell their crafts or garden harvest. A petting zoo will also be set up on these days. Call 647-2060 for more information.

Fairhaven Farmer's Market

Behind Village Books

Dates/Hours: Every Wednesday, 3pm-7pm, in the summer

Lynden Farmer's Market

Fourth St. and Grover St.

Dates/Hours: Every Saturday, 9am-1pm, in the summer

Lummi Island Farmer's Market

The Islander Store, 2106 S. Nugent Rd.
Dates/Hours: Every Saturday, 10:30am-12:30pm, in the summer

SUMMER

What a glorious time of the year. The weather is mild and the days are long. Take in a concert in a park or pick some of Whatcom County's notable berries.

Summer Concert Series

During the summer, free music concerts are held in Bellingham parks and at Western Washington University. Most of the concerts are family oriented and draw a large number of people who bring blankets, picnic lunches, and lawn chairs. For more information about the concerts in the parks, call the Bellingham Parks and Recreation Department at 676-6985. For more information about the concerts at Western Washington University, call 650-3000.

Boulevard Park Evening Concert Series

Schedule: Saturdays 7pm-9pm

These concerts take place in Boulevard Park and the setting couldn't be better. Enjoy the performance while the sun sets over Bellingham Bay. If you've lived in Whatcom County for any length of time, you're sure to see someone you know here. Staff from the Bellingham Parks and Recreation office lead children's games during these concerts. Parents are expected to supervise their children.

135

Bellingham Library Lawn
Brown Bag Concerts
Schedule: Fridays 12pm-1pm

These noon concerts are geared for children, and every Friday in the summer the library lawn is packed with families. The entertainers know that kids don't like to sit still very long so they encourage audience participation. Expect a lot of singing, clapping, and wiggling to the music. In case of rain, the concerts are held inside the Library Lecture Room. No, it's not quite as much fun then.

Elizabeth Park Concert Series
Schedule: Thursdays 6pm-8pm

The Eldridge Historical Society sponsors the concerts held in this beautiful neighborhood park. Pack an easy dinner, listen to the music, and let your kids play at the playground.

Western Washington University
Schedule: Wednesdays 12pm-1pm

These noon concerts are held in the Viking Union Plaza area and are attended by college students and families alike.

U-Pick Berry Farms

Whatcom County is famous for its berries. It produces more raspberries than any other county in the nation and leads the state in strawberry and blueberry production. Try some this summer. Many of the farms listed below also sell flats of pre-picked berries. Call before you go to confirm hours and berry availability.

Arneson's Berry Land

8808 Line Rd., Lynden; 354-4020
Hours: Monday-Saturday 8am-8pm. Closed Sunday.
Berries: Strawberries and raspberries

Boxx Berry Farm

6211 Northwest Rd., Ferndale; 384-4806
Hours: Monday-Saturday 10am-6pm. Closed Sunday.
Berries: Strawberries, raspberries, and blueberries

McPhail's Berry Farm

8318 Bob Hall Rd., Lynden; 354-5936
Hours: Every day 9am-6pm
Berries: Strawberries, raspberries, blackberries, boysenberries, and loganberries

McPhail's has a petting zoo full of friendly farm animals. They also put on a raspberry festival at the farm on the 3rd Saturday in July.

Mount's Strawberries

2318 Slater Rd., Ferndale; 384-0913
Hours: Every day 8:30am-7pm
Berries: Strawberries

Thompson's Berry Farm
5751 Lawrence Rd., Nugent Corner; 592-0964 or 592-5830
Berries: Raspberries, blueberries, marionberries

Van Diest Farm
8969 Jackman Rd., Lynden; 354-3818
Hours: Monday-Saturday 9am-7pm. Closed Sunday.
Berries: Strawberries

FALL

The air is crisp and the harvest is in. Celebrate by sampling autumn fruits at Cloud Mountain Farm or by picking your own pumpkin at Stoney Ridge Farm.

Cloud Mountain Farm
6906 Goodwin Rd., Everson; 966-5859

Date: First weekend in October
Hours: Saturday 10am-5pm; Sunday 12pm-5pm

Don't miss Cloud Mountain's Apple Festival which is held every fall during the first weekend in October. Families can sample over 100 varieties of farm-grown apples, pears, and grapes while listening to live music. Kids can make cider from an old-fashioned cider press or buy a pumpkin from Julia's Pumpkin Patch. Be sure to stop in the small store while you're at the festival. Apples, fresh cider, and local cheese are for sale. Last year, samples of dried apples (with or without caramel sauce) were also available.

Pumpkins are for sale during Cloud Mountain's Apple Festival. Photo courtesy of Cloud Mountain.

Stoney Ridge Farm
2092 VanDyk Rd., Everson; 966-3919

Dates: Every Thursday, Friday, and Saturday beginning in October.
Hours: 10am-5pm

When my family went to Stoney Ridge Farm for the first time, we were wowed by the sheer number of small children milling about. It turns out that Stoney Ridge is the quintessential field trip for nearly every preschool and kindergarten class in Whatcom County. Students come

139

to sample apples, pick pumpkins, and see the farm animals. My children loved watching all the other kids and we learned something, too. A group of students was hoisting a tin can up in the air by means of a pulley. When we looked up to see where the tin can was going, we noticed a ramp about twenty feet from the ground. The tin can went up and then dumped its contents into a bowl on that ramp. "Here come the goats!" the kids yelled. We looked, and sure enough, some goats were walking up, up, up that ramp to nibble on the goat food that had been dumped in their bowl. Of course, we had to try the pulley, too.

The goats are just one of the many kid attractions at Stoney Ridge. The other farm animals are another draw. Peacocks, chickens, bunnies, pigs, turkeys, sheep, and horses are all on display in well-kept pens. Stoney Ridge also has a simple playground for kids and a covered area with picnic tables set up. If your family wants to buy a pumpkin, you have two options. You can buy one already picked, or you can ride on a hay wagon and pick your own from the large pumpkin patch. Before you leave, be sure to stop by their Country Store. While you are browsing among the different kinds of apples, jam, and honey to purchase, your children can watch bees making a honeycomb. Adjacent to the store is a homey, casual cafe where customers can purchase large wedges of homemade apple or pumpkin pie, or apple slices with caramel sauce. Yum. The cafe also sells hot dogs, pop, coffee, and doughnuts. Stoney Ridge is a gem of a place. Plan on going at least once next October.

WINTER

The holiday season has begun. Make crafts at the Waldorf School's Holiday Faire, ride a Santa train, or cut down your own Christmas tree.

Whatcom Hills Waldorf School's Holiday Faire

941 Austin St., Bellingham; 733-3164

Date: Saturday before Thanksgiving
Hours: 10am-4pm

The Waldorf School's Holiday Faire is especially geared for children. High quality crafts such as wool felt gnomes or ornaments, beeswax candles, or hand sewn paper books can be made for a small fee. Families purchase tickets first for seventy-five cents a piece, and then these tickets are used to pay for the craft your child wishes to make. Kids as young as two years old could successfully make some of the crafts. I took my four year old. We bought ten tickets and had a wonderful time making beeswax candles and wooden candle holders to go with them, wool felt ornaments, and colorful stars made from translucent paper. Plan on eating while you're at the school. A cafe is set up in one of the buildings where there is always an abundance of delectable goodies, breads, and soups for sale.

Santa Train
Lake Whatcom Railway; 595-2218

Schedule: Call for specific times and dates
Cost: Adults $10; Children (under 18) $5

The Lake Whatcom Railway runs special Santa trains on Saturdays during the month of December. Sing Christmas carols, sip hot chocolate, and meet Santa. Be sure to dress warmly! The only heat in these vintage passenger cars comes from the passengers themselves. For more information on the Lake Whatcom Railway, see page 110.

Christmas Tree Farms

Listed below are places where your family can cut its own Christmas tree. Please call ahead to confirm hours and tree availability.

Alpine Meadow Tree Farm
3585 Valley Highway No. 9, Deming; 595-1019
Type of trees: Douglas, Fraser, Grand, Noble, Nordmann, Pine Balsam firs. Potted live trees.

Manthey's Christmas Treeland
773 W. Axton Rd., Ferndale; 384-0522
Type of trees: Douglas, Fraser, Grand, Noble, Nordmann, and Silver firs

Toys, Gifts & Clothes

If you're looking for toys, gifts, or clothes and don't want to head to the mall, try one of the following stores. They're locally owned, are pleasant to shop in, and often carry items that can't be found elsewhere in Whatcom County.

Academy Supplies
2915 Newmarket St., Bellingham; 676-5187

Hours: Monday-Saturday 10am-7pm; Sunday 11am-5pm

L ocal teachers shop here to buy materials for their class-rooms. This store is an excellent resource for parents as well. Academy Supplies carries educational puzzles and games, Brio toys, and Folkmanis puppets. They also carry Whatcom County's biggest selection of music for children. You can buy tapes and CDs from Bach to Raffi. Children's books, art supplies, and science kits are also for sale. Academy Supplies is a good place to find that just-right birthday present.

Fountain Super Drug
2416 Meridian St., Bellingham; 733-6200

Hours: Monday-Saturday 9am-10pm; Sunday 10am-7pm

T he first floor of Fountain Drug looks like an ordinary drug store. It has a pharmacy, greeting cards, magazines, and aspirin. However, when you descend the stairs to the basement, you are in for a big surprise. Dalton bone china, Brio toys, and Wilton cake decorating supplies are just some of the eclectic mix of items for sale. It's a wonderful place to poke around. Children will enjoy browsing in the toy section. Besides a huge selection of Brio toys, Fountain Drug carries Thomas trains, Breyer horses, stickers, books, games, puzzles, and science kits. Free gift wrapping is available. Take some time to explore the cake decorating aisles, too. Fountain Drug carries cake pans in a variety of shapes, along with the necessary decorating supplies. Innumerable plastic gee-gaws to put on top of cakes, pre-made sugar flowers, and other edible decorations are all for sale. You may become inspired here and never order a bakery cake again.

Kids Northwest
1421 Cornwall Ave., Bellingham; 676-6051

Hours: Monday-Friday 10am-5:30pm; Saturday 10am-5pm. Closed Sunday.

This friendly store carries high quality children's clothes and shoes with brands such as Patagonia, Flapdoodle, and Fresh Produce. It's a good place to buy durable seasonable items such as parkas, hats, mittens, and boots in the winter, and swimsuits, sandals, and sun hats in the summer. In the back of the store you can often find good bargains on the sale racks. A children's play area is also set up here.

Paper Dreams
1206 11th St., Bellingham; 676-8676

Hours: Monday-Saturday 10am-9pm; Sunday 12pm-5pm

Paper Dreams is a gift, card, and stationery store that also carries items that kids find fetching, such as candy, stickers, stuffed animals, and wacky toys. My kids like to come here to just look, although when they were younger it was hard not to touch everything. If you buy a book next door at Village Books and bring it over with your receipt, you can have it gift wrapped for free. A U.S. post office is located in the back of the store.

Yeager's Sporting Goods and Marine
3101 Northwest Ave., Bellingham; 733-1080

Hours: Monday-Thursday 9:30am-6pm; Friday 9:30am-7pm; Saturday 9am-5pm; Sunday 11am-4pm

When you walk into Yeager's you might not believe they even have a toy section. The main floor houses their sporting goods and marine section, and what you see are fishing poles, basketball nets, and camping equipment. Downstairs, however, lies a well-stocked toy department that takes up much of the lower floor. This is a good place to come for games, toy cars and trucks, models, Lego's, and one of the biggest selections of Playmobil in Whatcom County.

Activities
Listed by Region

To help you plan your outings more efficiently, I organized the places and activities listed in this book by region. That way, if you'd like to spend an afternoon poking around Ferndale, for instance, you'll know at a glance what activities are available there. Have fun and happy exploring!

BELLINGHAM
Downtown

Parks
Maritime Heritage Center

Museums
Bellingham Antique Radio
  Museum
Mindport
Whatcom Museum of
  History and Art
Arco Exhibits Building
Syre Education Center
Whatcom Children's
  Museum

Animals
Clark Feed & Seed
Hohl Feed & Seed

Indoor Activities
Tube Time
Whatcom Family YMCA

Books
Henderson Books

Arts & Crafts
Dakota Art Store

Buses
Whatcom Transit Center

Restaurants & Sweets
Avenue Bread
Bagelry
Bay City Ice Cream
Casa Que Pasa
Cookie Cafe
Mallard Ice Cream
Old Town
Pepper Sisters
Swan Cafe

Seasonal
Bellingham Farmer's
  Market
Bellingham Library Lawn
  Concerts

Clothes
Kids Northwest

BELLINGHAM
Fairhaven

Parks
Boulevard Park
Fairhaven Park
Marine Park

Indoor Activities
Bellingham Cruise
  Terminal

Outdoor Activities
Fairhaven Bike &
  Mountain Sport
Fairhaven Boat Works
Interurban Trail

Books
Village Books

Arts & Crafts
Bead Bazaar
Paint Expressions

Ferries & Trains
Amtrak Station
San Juan Island Commuter
San Juan Island Shuttle
  Express

Restaurants & Sweets
Abbey Garden Tea Room
The Colophon Cafe
Stanello's Restaurant

Seasonal Activities
Fairhaven Farmer's
  Market

Gifts & Cards
Paper Dreams

BELLINGHAM
Squalicum Harbor

Zuanich Point Park
Marine Life Center
Harbor Loop Promenade
Island Mariner Cruises

Squalicum Harbor boat
  launch
Trains along Roeder Ave.

FERNDALE

Ferndale Bakery
Hovander Homestead
  Park

Pioneer Park
Sardis Wildlife Center
Tennant Lake Interpretive
  Center

LUMMI ISLAND

Beach Store Cafe
Beach School
Islander Store

Lummi Island Overlook
Whatcom Chief Ferry

BLAINE/BIRCH BAY

Birch Bay State Park
Semiahmoo Park
Peace Arch State Park
Blaine Marine Park
Semiahmoo Mercantile
Birch Bay Waterslides

Blaine Harbor boat launch
The Plover
The Peace Train
The C Shop

LYNDEN

Berthusen Park

Lynden City Park

Pioneer Museum

Stremler Boekhandel

Lynden Dutch Bakery

Lynden Skateway

Lynden YMCA

EVERSON

Cloud Mountain Farm

Stoney Ridge Pumpkin Farm

SUMAS

Silver Lake Park

POINT ROBERTS

Lighthouse Marine Park

WICKERSHAM

Lake Whatcom Railway

Index